GAME CHANGER

PHIL LAWLER'S CRUSADE TO HELP CHILDREN BY IMPROVING PHYSICAL EDUCATION

GAME CHANGER

PHIL LAWLER'S CRUSADE TO HELP CHILDREN BY IMPROVING PHYSICAL EDUCATION

Ken Reed

Human Kinetics

Library of Congress Cataloging-in-Publication Data

Game changer : Phil Lawler's crusade to help children by improving physical education / PE4life.
    p. cm.
 ISBN-13: 978-1-4504-1345-9 (soft cover)
 ISBN-10: 1-4504-1345-5 (soft cover)
 1. Lawler, Phil. 2. Physical education teachers--United States--Biography. 3. Physical education for children--United States. 4. Physical fitness for children--United States. I. PE4life.
 GV333.L38G36 2011
 613.7'042--dc22

                        2011000848

ISBN-10: 1-4504-1345-5
ISBN-13: 978-1-4504-1345-9

Copyright © 2011 by PE4life

The web addresses cited in this text were current as of March 2011, unless otherwise noted.

Acquisitions Editor: Scott Wikgren; **Managing Editor:** Bethany J. Bentley; **Assistant Editors:** Derek Campbell and Rachel Brito; **Copyeditor:** Pat Connolly; **Graphic Designer:** Fred Starbird; **Graphic Artist:** Denise Lowry; **Cover Designer:** Keith Blomberg; **Photographs (cover and interior):** © Human Kinetics; **Photo Asset Manager:** Laura Fitch; **Photo Production Manager:** Jason Allen; **Art Manager:** Kelly Hendren; **Associate Art Manager:** Alan L. Wilborn; **Illustration:** © Human Kinetics; **Printer:** McNaughton & Gunn

A portion of the proceeds from sales of this book will go to the Lawler family.

Printed in the United States of America   10 9 8 7 6 5 4 3 2 1

The paper in this book is certified under a sustainable forestry program.

Human Kinetics
Website: www.HumanKinetics.com

United States: Human Kinetics, P.O. Box 5076, Champaign, IL 61825-5076
800-747-4457
e-mail: humank@hkusa.com

Canada: Human Kinetics, 475 Devonshire Road Unit 100, Windsor, ON N8Y 2L5
800-465-7301 (in Canada only)
e-mail: info@hkcanada.com

Europe: Human Kinetics, 107 Bradford Road, Stanningley, Leeds LS28 6AT, United Kingdom
+44 (0) 113 255 5665
e-mail: hk@hkeurope.com

Australia: Human Kinetics, 57A Price Avenue, Lower Mitcham, South Australia 506
08 8372 0999
e-mail: info@hkaustralia.com

New Zealand: Human Kinetics, P.O. Box 80, Torrens Park, South Australia 5062
0800 222 062
e-mail: info@hknewzealand.com

E5520

"It's about enabling each student to maintain a physically active lifestyle forever. It means emphasizing fitness and well-being, not athleticism. It eliminates practices that humiliate students. And it assesses students on their progress in reaching personal physical activity and fitness goals. A quality PE program exposes kids to the fun and long-term benefits of movement—it's really that simple."

—*Phil Lawler*

CONTENTS

FOREWORD

By
Dr. Kenneth Cooper

There's no way to dance around it: The state of our kids' physical fitness has never been worse than it is today. As a physician who's often referred to as "The Father of Aerobics" and who's spent most of my professional life encouraging people to move, that's depressing news indeed.

Over 75 percent of U.S. children are not active even 20 minutes a day, the minimum daily activity requirement. We *must* get our kids moving. But just as important, we need to educate our young people about the importance of staying physically active for a lifetime—not just for today, this week, or this semester. I can think of no better way to do this than through high-quality physical education (PE) programs that are based on health and wellness.

Students at schools with daily fitness-oriented physical education programs are reaping the benefits of being physically fit: (1) improved health; (2) higher academic performance; and (3) fewer behavioral problems. There's more good news. Exercise has also been shown to improve attention span and focus, to lower anxiety and depression levels, and to raise self-esteem.

However, to reap all these benefits, our physical education programs must evolve from the "old school" model centered on team sports, of which most of us are familiar. To maximize the benefits of physical education, PE curriculums and philosophies must become more health and wellness based. The emphasis needs to be on individualized fitness goals and programs for *every* student, not just the athletically inclined. This is the "New PE."

This cause is dear to my heart. I've spent the majority of my career trying to educate and motivate adults to exercise. It's been an extremely tough challenge because it's difficult to break long-ingrained habits of inactivity. But studies show that children who exercise regularly are likely to continue to do so as adults. Therefore, we need to reach our kids with the messages of the "New PE."

Nobody understood this better and lived it more completely than Phil Lawler, the focus of this book. Lawler was the "Father of the New PE" and a legend in the health-and-wellness-based physical education movement. Lawler and his colleagues in the Naperville (Illinois) 203 school district developed a true state-of-the-art physical education program.

The students at Naperville 203 consistently score higher than their peers across the country on standardized fitness assessments. The percentage of overweight students in this school district is consistently 5 percent or less, compared to the national average of 30 percent.

The benefits of physical fitness are also being seen in Naperville's classrooms. For example, Naperville Central High School students who took a fitness-based physical education course, in addition to a literacy class, improved their reading and comprehension scores by 1.4 years on a grade-level equivalency scale. This was nearly a 50 percent greater improvement than students who took the literacy class alone.

Today, Naperville Central counselors encourage their students to take their toughest class immediately after physical education.

The poor state of physical fitness among our youth is more than an educational issue. It's a major health care issue for this country. This is the first generation of children in more than 100 years that is expected to have a shorter lifespan than its predecessor. Rates of diabetes, cardiovascular disease, and other health problems among teenagers in this country are skyrocketing. At the current pace, health care costs will undoubtedly bankrupt the United States.

Phil Lawler's growing army of physical education revolutionaries might be the only thing that can save us. In my eyes, Phil Lawler was a true hero. He was the most important person in the world in the area of improving physical education in our schools. He positively affected thousands of students, and the movement that he started will make millions of lives better in the coming years.

As you'll discover in this book, everyone can contribute to this movement. I sincerely and passionately urge you to thoughtfully consider how you can make a difference in this effort within your realm of influence.

Our children are counting on us.

Dr. Kenneth H. Cooper
Cooper Aerobics Center
Dallas, Texas

PREFACE

This is a story about an ordinary man who became a hero. It's about a teacher who had an epiphany that changed not only his career but also his life. It's about his passion for helping kids and how that passion allowed him to summon the courage to buck the status quo. It's also about all the people he inspired by addressing their hearts as much as their minds.

It's a story about Phil Lawler, a man who played a leading role in getting the United States—and in recent years, countries around the globe—closer to a significant paradigm shift in education. And in the end, it's a story about a man whose work and dedication will end up dramatically improving the lives of millions of young people.

It's certainly a story with humble beginnings. Lawler spent most of his career as a physical education teacher at a junior high school in the small bedroom community of Naperville, Illinois. In the middle of his career, he transitioned from a sport-obsessed gym teacher whose focus was coaching baseball, to a premier physical educator whose mission was getting kids physically active—all kids, not just the athletically inclined—in order to enhance their overall wellness for a lifetime.

The story follows Lawler as a worldwide movement—spurred to a large degree by Lawler's tireless efforts—emerges from its embryonic stage and is poised to take off. The movement gains momentum as powerful research about exercise's positive impact on the brain emerges.

This isn't a book driven by facts and figures but instead by the human factor behind the movement, especially the flesh-and-blood hero at its epicenter. It's not a biography in the traditional sense but a story about how one person—if fueled by passion—can make a difference that expands in many directions.

To know Phil Lawler was to be inspired by his drive to make the world a better place. We hope that this book gives you a glimpse of Lawler's light and how it energized an important revolution in the world of education.

PROLOGUE

The Epiphany

Phil Lawler walked into Madison Junior High School in Naperville, Illinois, on a bright sunny morning in the spring of 1989. He said hello to several colleagues. Then he began to get ready for the six physical education classes he would teach that day before heading to Naperville Central High School to tutor the pitchers on the school's baseball team.

For Lawler, a veteran physical education teacher and coach, the day had started like most days. But this day would prove to be very different.

It was "Mile Run Day" in the Madison PE department. Many of the students hated the mile run, but they had learned to tolerate—if not accept—it.

A year earlier, Lawler and his two fellow PE teachers, Mike Crackel and Carol Vermaat, had decided to institute a weekly mile run.

"Mike brought in an article to our staff meeting one day that highlighted the decline in the health of American children," said Lawler. "We talked about it for a while and discussed how, as physical education teachers, we should be in a position to help do something about it. Then, all of a sudden, Mike said we should institute a mile run to get our kids more fit. Carol and I laughed, thinking he was joking. He wasn't, and the more we talked about it, the more we all thought it was a good idea."

The trio faced plenty of opposition to their mile run concept. Many students and parents, as well as several Madison teachers, thought that making students run a mile for time wasn't appropriate. A lot of them voiced their displeasure—formally and informally—with what they saw as a boot-camp-like activity. Running a mile—for time—was a significant departure from the department's traditional routine of team sports, skill development, and games.

Lawler was the stereotypical PE teacher and coach. He admittedly got into physical education because he thought it was the best path toward a coaching career. In essence, for much of the first half of his career, he was simply a team sport coach who ran PE classes before practices started after school.

On Mile Run Day, he'd grab his whistle and stopwatch, put them around his neck, and head out to the field—just like every other coach and PE instructor you may recall from your school days or may remember seeing in old movies.

As the boys and girls went by his post, about halfway along the course, he would do his best job of "motivating" them by barking out "Pick up the pace!" or "Push it a little! I know you can work harder than that!"

"I thought I could tell by observation which students were working hard and which weren't," said Lawler. "I felt it was my job to motivate the students I thought needed motivating."

A few weeks before this particular day's mile run, Lawler had picked up a newfangled device called a heart rate monitor. He'd been told that it was a new way to measure the effort of his students. So, on this particular day, he had decided to put the heart rate monitor on a slender girl who seemed to be averse to exercise and consistently finished near the rear during the mile run. She wasn't overweight and didn't have asthma or any other apparent health problem. Lawler thought her problem was simply a lack of interest and self-motivation. In short, he thought she was lazy.

"This young lady was not athletic at all, showed no interest in physical education, and acted like the last thing she wanted to do in the world was sweat," said Lawler. "Whatever we did, she was always walking or jogging *very* slowly. She appeared to not be pushing herself at all. I thought the heart rate monitor would verify my suspicions about her lack of effort."

True to form, this 13-year-old girl once again finished the mile in the back of the pack.

"She walked—maybe jogged a little bit—for the entire mile," explained Lawler. "She finished in 13 1/2 minutes. Most days I would've been encouraging her to push herself more, but on this day, I just let her finish. I fully expected that the heart rate monitor would show that she wasn't putting out any effort.

"Well, after class I downloaded the heart rate monitor on the computer, fully expecting it to confirm my observation that this girl was not expending any energy during the mile," continued Lawler. "What I discovered, however, was that she had an average heart rate of 187 and that she'd peaked at 207 at the finish line. By my observation she wasn't doing anything, but in reality, she was working *too* hard.

"I was sitting at the computer, staring at the screen, and the lightbulb went on like a big flash. I thought to myself, *Boy, we've screwed this mile run thing up royally. We have no idea how hard these kids are working based on our eyes and stopwatches.* I started thinking back to all the kids we must have turned off to exercise because we weren't able to give them credit for their effort."

Lawler's eyes had lied to him. He was convinced this girl was lazy and not pushing herself enough. In reality, she was working harder than the majority of kids in Lawler's PE class, including the top athletes.

Twenty years later, Lawler leaned back in his chair and reflected on what he learned on that fateful day.

"This girl was at the bottom of the class based on the old criteria, but if I had a heart rate monitor on every kid in class that day, it might've turned out that she was at the top of the class in terms of effort," said Lawler. "She could've been the hardest working kid we had in class on that particular day.

"In those days, we basically said, 'If you can't run a mile under eight minutes, you're a failure.' What our eyes and stopwatches didn't tell us then was how hard kids were actually working. Heart rate monitors can tell us that. That was an absolutely huge day for us. The old way of evaluation—observation and a stopwatch—was not valid. We were judging—and grading—based on the question 'How fast did you run it?' It was based on athletic performance, not a fitness assessment."

In fact, while staring at the girl's heart rate numbers on the computer screen that day, Lawler had an epiphany that would change the entire course of his life.

As Lawler drove to baseball practice that afternoon, he realized that he had to completely change his approach to physical education. He knew that he needed to make PE more fitness based and needed to start grading students more on effort than outcomes. His heart told him that he had a moral responsibility to do what he could to change the way physical education was taught.

What he didn't know while driving to Central's baseball field that day was just how far his new quest would take him—or the impact he would ultimately have on students, teachers, administrators, parents, doctors, professors, researchers, and business leaders.

What he did know was that he could no longer teach PE the same old way anymore.

Lawler's life would never again be the same. His passionate quest to change physical education had begun.

A STEREOTYPICAL PHYSICAL EDUCATION TEACHER AND COACH

"**C**oming out of college, I wanted to be a coach, especially a baseball coach. At the time, I just looked at teaching as a means to an end. It was something I needed to do in order to coach. That was my mindset. I don't like admitting that but it's the truth."

—*Phil Lawler*

Philip R. Lawler was born February 18, 1950, on a farm near Carroll, Iowa, a small farming community in northwest Iowa. He was one of six siblings, all born within seven years of each other. Phil was child number five, one of four boys.

His dad only had an eighth grade education but deeply valued education and fervently stressed its importance to his children. More than anything, however, he valued family, a strong work ethic, and working together to do what needed to be done. The Lawlers farmed beans, corn, and oats. They also had cattle and hogs on their Iowa farm.

"My parents constantly stressed to me and my brothers and sisters—by their words and actions—whatever you do, do well," said Lawler.

My parents constantly stressed to me and my brothers and sisters—by their words and actions—whatever you do, do well.

Lawler's older brother Dan described the family ethic this way: "If it's worth doing, do it right. We didn't just believe that, we all lived it every day on the farm."

Phil agreed and then added another lesson that he picked up back on the farm.

"There was an element of my father's philosophy that said, 'Don't be satisfied with the status quo. If there's a better way to do something, do it. Don't shy away because of hard work, or because others don't share your values. If you really think you're right, take it on no matter what others think.' I like to think I've adopted that approach to life."

"We learned the value of teamwork, of working together on a common cause," says Dan Lawler. "Everybody contributed something on the farm. We worked hard, and we learned what it means to be part of a whole."

It wasn't all work on the farm, however. Sports, especially baseball, became a popular diversion.

"Dad cut out a baseball field on our farm," said Lawler. "It helped bond our family together. I played four sports in school, but baseball is the one ingrained in me. It was the only sport my dad played. As a result, I think it became the sport our family knew the most about."

It's little wonder that *Field of Dreams,* a baseball movie starring Kevin Costner and set in Iowa on a farm, was Lawler's favorite movie. Costner's character cuts a baseball field out of the cornstalks on his farm and reflects throughout the movie on the simpler things in life, such as playing catch with your father.

Baseball became Lawler's career of choice. Although he was a very good baseball player himself, he realized that his chances of a pro baseball career were slim. Thus, he turned his attention to coaching.

"I wanted to coach, particularly baseball," said Lawler. "I realized in high school that becoming a teacher was the best path for becoming a baseball coach. I was told that becoming a physical education or social studies teacher provided the easiest path for coaching.

"Well, PE made sense as a pathway for coaching, but I wasn't sure what social studies had to do with coaching," said Lawler. "When I asked about it, I was told you could always turn on a movie as a social studies teacher and then work on your coaching."

Lawler let out a hearty laugh in recollection. "That sounds horrible now. But at the time, where my mind-set was then—focused on coaching not teaching—it made perfect sense."

As a senior at Wall Lake Community High School, a small school with 78 students total (9th through 12th grade), Lawler worked on the yearbook, sang in the choir, and played four sports. Somehow, he also found time to begin attending Future Teachers of America (FTA) meetings. The Wall Lake community was so quaint and innocent that as part of the FTA program, Lawler did some substitute teaching in the local elementary school while still in high school.

The FTA experience convinced Lawler that his calling was to teach and coach. Education has been a popular career path for the Lawler family. Of the six Lawler kids, five pursued careers in education, and four became coaches. In addition, several of the Lawler siblings have children who are now teachers.

"After high school, I went to Buena Vista College in Storm Lake, Iowa," recalled Lawler. "I had a double major in PE and history—history in case I found an opening for a social studies teacher. Coaching was still priority number one."

Lawler landed his first teaching position in 1973. It was at a small high school in little Marathon, Iowa. The high school had 68 students spread over four grades. Lawler felt right at home.

"I was the assistant football coach and head girls softball coach—in the same fall season!" said Lawler. "After that year, I moved on to a job in Manning, Iowa, for two years. I wasn't a very good teacher in either place. I showed a lot of films in class."

His big break came in 1976 when he landed a job in Naperville, Illinois, a nice suburban community near Chicago. The Naperville schools were much bigger than what he had experienced in Iowa.

"I talked myself into a job that was half-time social studies teacher and part-time trainer and school bus driver," said Lawler. "I coached football and baseball. I made it through that year and made enough connections so that I was hired at Madison Junior High School as a PE teacher and athletic director. It was a brand-new school, and I was the first teacher hired. I was hired even before the school had a principal."

Lawler taught physical education for 30 years, but he claimed that he wasn't an effective PE teacher for the first 15.

"Early in my career, I really didn't teach PE properly," said Lawler. "In fact, I did almost everything wrong. I had the students play dodgeball, where the big, athletic kids could humiliate the nonathletic kids. I used exercise as punishment instead of a way to build fitness levels. We intimidated. I ran PE classes with a disciplined, militaristic sports model. I lived by advice I received early in my career: 'Don't ever smile the first semester. That way students will see that you're strong, not weak.' I focused on team sports. In short, everything I lecture against today I did early in my career. If there's a wrong way to do something, I did it."

Lawler said that one of the things he did especially poorly was the grading of students.

"My classes ran very smoothly, but I'm not sure if there was any real education going on. Our main grading policy was, Did they change clothes? Did they shower? Did they comply with what we asked without complaining? If they dressed for class and participated, they got a good grade. That said, I'd also grade on team sport skills. For example, in football, I graded them on how far they could pass and punt. Crazy huh? Most of my kids never played football or had any desire to play football. I consider myself a very ineffective teacher during those times.

"I'm not proud of it," said Lawler. "But the truth is, I wasn't a very good teacher during the early part of my career. It was all sports and coaching for me."

Lawler said that if you look at the history of physical education in the United States, it's easy to understand how the traditional model of PE came to be.

"Physical education became part of America's school system for military readiness reasons around World War I," said Lawler. "PE was a big focus again at the time of World War II. Apart from war times, the focus became sports readiness. It was the sports model of PE. The only reason to have PE was to teach sports to our kids. I believe 99 percent of PE teachers in the '60s, '70s, and '80s were athletes or those interested in sports."

According to Lawler, expectations for PE teachers had long centered on sport performance rather than education.

"When it came to PE, there was no accountability," said Lawler of what he called the "old way" or the Old PE. "Principals were interested in two things: (1) That nobody got hurt in PE; and (2) Be a successful coach after school; that is, win games."

Despite Lawler's self-deprecating nature when it came to discussing his early teaching career, he wasn't a bad teacher given the times. Unlike some sport-oriented PE teachers, Lawler didn't simply roll out the ball in PE class and then read the sports page or work on a game plan for that weekend's game. He sincerely believed in the value of team sports and wanted to teach sport skills to as many kids as possible. He would work tirelessly with all his students—regardless of athletic ability—on how to shoot a layup in basketball or swing a bat in softball. He wanted all students to reap the same benefits and pleasures from sports that he had.

Meanwhile, his passion for coaching only increased. He studied everything he could get his hands on about the art and science of coaching. Although he coached several sports—baseball, basketball, football, and track—in his early years, baseball was his true love. And it would be baseball that he would focus on.

Lawler narrowed his focus to pitching. He quickly became an expert in pitching technique and strategy. It wasn't long before he was widely known throughout high school baseball circles in Illinois as somewhat of a pitching guru. From day one of his career, Lawler was passionate about baseball and his coaching responsibilities.

But admittedly, he didn't put the same passion and intensity into his PE teaching. It wasn't until an innocent staff meeting with his PE colleagues at Madison Junior High that he began to see his role as a physical education teacher differently.

2

THE BEGINNING OF THE NEW PHYSICAL EDUCATION

> **"I** haven't seen anything as uplifting and inspiring as Naperville's program in decades."
>
> —Dr. John J. Ratey, MD, author of SPARK: The Revolutionary New Science of Exercise and the Brain

It started out like every other staff meeting they'd gone through—a little small talk centered on the prior night's sport results, recent family activities, and school politics. About 10 minutes into the meeting, Mike Crackel, Madison Junior High School physical education teacher, pulled out a newspaper article on the declining health of children in the United States. According to the article, American kids were getting heavier and unhealthier.

This was 1988. At the time, Crackel, Lawler, and Carol Vermaat were typical physical education teachers: Teach one sport for a two-week unit and then switch to another sport for the next two-week unit. For a change of pace, mix in a little dodgeball. They were definitely the standard "old school" gym teachers. Even so, they always tried to be innovative.

"We tried something new every year," said Lawler. "We were a creative department, a creative staff. I remember one year we put in a bicycle unit, which ended with a bicycle rodeo. The kids loved it."

"We liked change," said Vermaat. "Our goal was to try something new in the curriculum each year. We were always talking about new ideas and asking, 'What are other people doing?' We did things like golf and archery that were actually cutting edge at the time."

But they'd never really thought about health and wellness, or about putting more emphasis on physical fitness in their classes.

Crackel's article got them thinking along those lines.

"Here we were physical education teachers, and the health of our nation's kids was declining," said Lawler. "We looked at each other and said, 'We should do something about this. We could make a difference.'

"In looking back, it was the article Mike Crackel brought in to our meeting—and the discussion we had about it—that became the cornerstone of the new way we approached physical education."

The first step of the transformation was pretty basic. The trio decided to focus a little more on cardiovascular fitness in class, emphasize the Presidential Physical Fitness Award, and do a mile run twice a year. In addition, they gradually deemphasized or dropped activities from their curriculum that had only limited fitness benefits and involved a lot of standing around.

"Gradually, we became more and more committed to a fitness focus," said Lawler. "At our meetings we started talking more about focusing on cardiovascular fitness."

At one staff meeting, they spent a little time talking about what to name their new approach.

"The 'New Math' curriculum was getting a lot of publicity about this time, so when we were talking about what to call our new PE curriculum, Mike Crackel said, 'Let's call it the New PE,'" said Vermaat. "It stuck."

"Fairly quickly, we concluded that if we were going to do this New PE stuff, PE with a fitness focus, we had to go all the way," said Lawler. "For example, we decided that running the mile twice a year wasn't going to help students improve their times or get more fit. We decided—with Crackel's urging—to implement a weekly mile run. That set off some fireworks! We started getting letters from parents saying we were torturing students by making them run the mile every week!"

In fact, after their decision to implement a weekly mile run, the Madison Junior High School physical education staff was inundated with protests from every angle. Many students vociferously stated their opinions against the new policy. On Mile Run Day, there was sure to be a line of kids outside the school nurse's office with reasons why they couldn't participate. Parents were nearly as upset, many of them regularly sending notes to school asking that their child be excused from the mile run for a variety of reasons. Even a few teachers on staff expressed dismay with the new fitness regimen.

Nevertheless, the PE staff was steadfast in their belief that they were doing the right thing.

"With our new fitness and wellness emphasis, things like the number of layups you could make in 30 seconds became pointless," says Vermaat.

"It was about this time that I first asked myself, 'What is it like to be a student with no interest in sports and have to walk into PE class?'" said

Lawler. "I never thought about how painful that might be for students that weren't athletically inclined."

Shortly after implementing the mile run, Lawler and his colleagues began doing regular body fat composition testing. This only added to the consternation of a significant number of Madison parents.

Fortunately, the physical education team received strong support from the school's administration, and that was enough to ward off rebellion efforts that gradually dissipated over a couple years.

"Well, we had plenty of students and parents that resisted the new approach to physical education," recalls Jerry Virgo, Madison Junior High School principal from 1980 to 1999. "We tried to be very open with parents. We listened to their complaints and then tried to defuse the emotional aspects and focus on the practical aspects of the issue. We calmly explained that we weren't trying to embarrass their child. We stressed that we were trying to give the kids a better understanding of the health benefits of fitness and how that understanding could carry into their adult lives."

No revolutions are easy—especially at the beginning.

"The actual beginning of this New PE movement really started with the weekly mile run, and we ran it religiously," said Lawler. "It developed a reputation, and it took a couple years of students going through the program before everyone finally realized we were serious and the rebellion stopped.

"We finally started getting new classes of kids coming to Madison that knew, and accepted, that a weekly mile run is what happens when you go to Madison. We had elementary teachers starting to work their students harder and telling them 'This is what happens when you go to Madison.' It was quite the battle, but we persevered because we truly believed we were doing the right thing."

Heart Rate Monitors: The Next Big Breakthrough

Lawler thought that using a stopwatch to time every kid in the mile run made sense as an evaluation tool. He thought he was doing the right thing by "eyeballing" the students to determine the effort they were giving. And he thought he was on the right path by pushing the kids he didn't think were running hard enough.

All that changed when he discovered the heart rate monitor and started using one in his PE classes. Today, the heart rate monitor holds a prominent position in the Naperville 203 physical education program, but it had a rather inauspicious beginning.

In retrospect, it was a door prize that Lawler "won" that ignited the New PE program at Naperville.

Lawler and a couple PE colleagues—Paul Zientarski, a physical education teacher at Naperville Central High School, and Dave Bucher, a physical education teacher at Naperville North High School—created a conference in 1985 for physical education teachers in the Naperville area. This conference was called the DuPage County Physical Education Institute. It took place annually at the end of February or early March.

In later years, the conference would become extremely popular, drawing attendees from all over the state and region. Today, in fact, attendees come from almost every state in the nation and from multiple countries. But early on, Lawler and his colleagues struggled to get PE teachers to attend—and once there, to get them to stay until the end of the program.

In preparation for the fourth annual conference in 1989, Lawler was in charge of finding vendors that might sponsor the conference, or a particular session, and maybe provide a door prize as well. Lawler was particularly interested in getting door prizes that he could use to entice the teachers to stay for the entire day's activities.

"The first couple years, we did pretty well rounding up people to attend the conference, but they gradually started to disappear as the day wore on," recalled Lawler. "If we came up with some decent door prizes—basketballs, footballs, jump ropes, water bottles, etc.—and didn't draw for them until the end of the day, we could keep our attendance up pretty well for the entire conference."

One day, while going through the door prizes he'd collected for the conference, Lawler came across a heart rate monitor that one vendor had given him. Although he'd read and heard a little about heart rate monitors and their benefits, he'd never actually seen one or spent any time thinking about getting one for himself or his students.

Nevertheless, he was intrigued by the heart rate monitor, and he thought it might be a fun, creative toy for his PE department. He spontaneously decided to "award" himself this particular door prize.

"This is one of those stories you tend to keep in the closet. I put the heart rate monitor to the side and said to myself, 'I'm not giving this heart rate monitor away. I worked too hard trying to put this conference on. Phil Lawler just won this door prize,'" said Lawler. "I'd read a little about heart rate monitors and what they could do, so I thought I'd play around with one on our students."

The heart rate monitor that Lawler "won" was ultimately used during the mile run on the unsuspecting 13-year-old girl he thought was the laziest kid in his class. It turns out she was one of the hardest working. This was the day that Lawler had an epiphany about what PE was and what it could be (see "Prologue").

Even though the girl was walking and it took her 13.5 minutes to finish the mile, her average heart rate was 187. She peaked at 207 at the finish line.

After Lawler got over his shock regarding what the data from the heart rate monitor were telling him, he became completely enamored with what heart rate monitors could mean to physical education. He realized that using a stopwatch and his eyes to evaluate his students during the mile run wasn't a very effective means of evaluation.

"When I saw that the student I thought was one of the laziest in class was actually one of the hardest working, I realized that heart rate monitors could tell me stuff that my eyes and years of experience as a physical education teacher and coach couldn't," said Lawler. "The girl I thought was working the least was actually one of our hardest working students. I was completely wrong to assume she was being lazy, and I didn't know it until I read her heart rate monitor data. With the heart rate monitor, we could now measure effort. It was one of our first big breakthroughs."

In particular, Lawler saw how heart rate monitors could level the playing field for his students, athletic and nonathletic alike. The monitors were

HEART RATE MONITORS

Heart rate is a guide for gauging exercise intensity. Heart rate provides students with feedback to assist them in monitoring how hard they are working and helps them stay in their target heart rate zone (THZ). Although experts agree that children don't necessarily have to work in a certain THZ to reap the benefits of physical activity, the value of teaching students about target heart rate (THR) is to help them understand the concept of exercise intensity and the health benefits of physical activity.

By measuring time spent working in the THZ in physical education class, teachers can assess if the student has maintained an activity level that will enhance cardiovascular fitness; they can also monitor the student's progress. This holds the students accountable for their own intensity levels and allows the teacher to grade the students' performance.

What is the appropriate heart rate zone for adolescents?

Although there are no formulas designed specifically for children or early adolescents, the following can be used as a guide to determine target heart rate zone (THZ).

Threshold (lower end) of target heart rate zone = (220 – age) × .6

Upper end of target heart rate zone = (220 – age) × .85

Target HR 60-85%

Age	Lower end of training zone	Upper end of training zone
11	125	178
12	125	177
13	124	176
14	124	175
15	123	174

(continued)

Heart Rate Monitors (continued)

Approximately 60 to 85 percent of maximum heart rate is the prime zone for moderate to vigorous physical activity. Keep in mind that the error range of either formula for THZ is plus or minus 20 beats because of the assumption that 220 is everyone's maximum heart rate at birth.

How can heart rate be calculated?

Heart rate can be taken manually by placing two fingers on one of the carotid arteries in the neck and counting the number of times a beat is felt in a 15-second time period. That number is multiplied by 4 to determine the heart rate in beats per minute (BPM). For example, a 15-second carotid pulse count of 24 equates to the following formula: $24 \times 4 = 96$ BPM.

Are there any other ways to measure heart rate?

Heart rate monitors can also be used to measure heart rate. These are personal monitoring devices that allow people to measure their heart rate in real time or record their heart rate for later review. Heart rate monitors consist of two elements that sync together: a chest strap transmitter and a wrist receiver.

Why should we monitor heart rate?

Students can be graded on staying in their target heart rate zone (THZ) for an optimum amount of time. Being able to monitor students' progress allows teachers to report progress and measurable outcomes of a fitness program.

Information originally compiled and provided by PE4life for The Century Council's Ask Listen Learn interactive game release and appeared in the game's facilitator's guide.

a fair measure of effort, whether a student was an elite basketball player or a clumsy out-of-shape kid who hated team sports. Both kids could conceivably be in the "healthy fitness zone" on the heart rate monitor no matter how fast they were running. And the monitors allowed students to develop fitness plans customized for their own bodies.

Rick Schupbach, a PE teacher at the PE4life Academy Training Center in Grundy Center, Iowa, firmly believes that the heart rate monitor levels the playing field for all students.

"When we used to tell the overweight kid to speed up and catch the others as they were doing something like running, we now have the monitor and tell them to stay within his or her limits," says Schupbach. "The accountability we have to our students is very exciting."

"The heart rate monitor taught me that I could treat kids as individuals, not masses," says Zientarski. "The slow kids could now get *A*s for walking, slowing down, and staying in the target zone."

Lawler was so excited about what heart rate monitors could mean for his program that he embarked on a quest to increase Madison Junior High's supply. One monitor wasn't going to cut it. He wanted to be able to put a heart rate monitor on every kid in class.

"Phil became fanatical about heart rate monitors and wanting to increase our supply," said Vermaat. "As I said, we liked change. That particular year our change was incorporating heart rate monitors."

"I had never heard Phil complain about his job—ever," says Lawler's wife, Denise Lawler. "But when he discovered the heart rate monitor and started on his New PE path, it reinvigorated his career. He loved talking to people about the New PE."

Lawler and his colleagues began to add additional heart rate monitors to their supply as their budget and creativity allowed. First, it was one heart rate monitor for the boys and one for the girls, and it gradually grew from there.

One key event that increased the Madison staff's motivation regarding heart rate monitors was the appearance of Beth Kirkpatrick—a Grundy Center, Iowa, physical education teacher—as a keynote speaker at that year's DuPage County PE Institute. Kirkpatrick was a passionate and innovative PE teacher who had been experimenting with heart rate monitors for some time and realized the tremendous value they represented for PE teachers. At the conference, she shared the growing mound of heart rate monitor data she had collected from her students in Iowa. She also talked about how the regular use of heart rate monitors had dramatically improved students' fitness levels.

Kirkpatrick, an energetic and passionate physical education professional, is commonly viewed as the first PE teacher to regularly, systematically, and scientifically use heart rate monitors in K-12 physical education. Interestingly, Kirkpatrick's story of how her entire approach to physical education changed is similar to Lawler's epiphany—and every bit as powerful.

"The wakeup call for me came after I had been teaching physical education for seven years," says Kirkpatrick. "I was also the head basketball coach. I was doing very traditional physical education, with sports as the model—two weeks of soccer, volleyball, etc. I put people on teams at night and would have them play each other in a tournament the next day. That's how I thought PE should be.

"Well, one day we were doing the mile run, and I was doing cardio counts with a stopwatch. I was yelling at the last three or four kids, each of whom was obese. I was screaming and yelling because I was worried about finishing before the class period was over. We only had 48 minutes. I was yelling at the last kids, screaming at them to finish.

"When I look back on this, I wasn't concerned about them, what might be going on in their bodies or minds. I was just concerned about getting them dressed on time! At that point in my career, I don't even remember pulling an obese kid aside and really talking to her about anything of substance. I was always talking to the athletes. My whole thought process was athletics.

"Anyway, I was screaming at this poor girl, 'Why can't you run that part? Run around the curve! Run!' She started running, and she collapsed right in front of me. I thought she was dead. As I'm running over to do CPR, I'm thinking, *What did I do? I didn't mean to do it. I'm sorry.* Then I started making all these promises to God. *Don't let her die. I'll never do it again. I'm sorry.* I'm thinking all that to myself within a few seconds. When you've made a horrible mistake, you wish you could have it back.

"When I got to her, I turned her over, and she came to. She had just passed out. She wasn't dead! The first thing she said to me was, 'I'm so sorry. I know I hold up the whole class. I know you're mad at me.' She was apologizing to me! I couldn't say anything. But I knew there were so many wrongs about her apologizing to me.

"As I helped her up, I saw that there was blood coming down the side of her leg. I thought she had cut herself when she fell. I said, 'Why are you bleeding?' She said, 'I have a blood blister. I always get that when I run this mile.' Her legs were so heavy that they rubbed against each other and started bleeding because she was moving as fast as she could for 15 minutes—even though others were finishing in 8 or 9 minutes. The whole time she's chasing them, and bleeding.

"I'm thinking as I'm walking in, *What kind of a day is this for her?* She's sweating—her whole T-shirt is wringing wet. You can see the outline of her large body, including large breasts, large stomach, thighs—mortifying to a girl, and I suppose a boy, as well. Her hair is completely wringing wet. God knows what her heart rate was.

"We're putting our obese kids and our asthma kids, unknowingly, unwittingly, through exercise abuse. It doesn't have to be that way. There's a much better way with heart rate monitors. We shouldn't be trying to do cardio testing with stopwatches. We're using third world technology to test kids in the United States—third world technology!

"My whole mission in life has been to correct that day, to make sure something like that doesn't happen again.

"I always say *I was mentally ill* in those days . . . but, you can recover."

Kirkpatrick's presentation at the 1990 DuPage Institute helped spur the Madison PE contingent to continue down their "fitness first" path and to make heart rate monitors a key component of their New PE curriculum. Lawler and his team believed that with heart rate monitors they could actually understand what was going on inside their students' bodies, rather than go by what their eyeballs and stopwatches were telling them. Their new goal was to acquire enough heart rate monitors to equip an entire class.

Lawler moved from having 2 monitors to 6, and then 15. Within a year, through budget modifications and creative fund-raising efforts—including reaching out to parents and the community—Madison Junior High had accumulated 30 heart rate monitors. At that point, Lawler, Crackel, and Vermaat would alternate using the heart rate monitors with their respective classes.

One of the great positives of the heart rate monitors—from the perspective of students, parents, and teachers—was that the monitors allowed kids to be graded on effort instead of athletic ability. For the first time at Madison, students could achieve an *A* without having great times in the mile run or exhibiting outstanding sport skills. Students found that if they consistently kept their heart rates in the target zone—meaning they were giving the required effort for fitness gains—they were well on their way to an *A* in physical education.

"I was really excited about heart rate monitors because I could see they were the great equalizer," said Lawler. "I thought it was a way to help reach the kids that hated PE because they weren't as athletic as some of their classmates. I remember a mother once telling me—with tears in her eyes—about what a bad experience PE was for her going through school, how humiliating it was and how much she dreaded it. I saw heart rate monitors as a way to help students like that—to help them be evaluated on their effort and not their athletic ability."

Another Breakthrough: Small-Sided Games

As they added heart rate monitors, the trio of Lawler, Vermaat, and Crackel continued to increasingly emphasize cardiovascular fitness in their curriculum.

However, once they had enough heart rate monitors to equip an entire class, they discovered that although their students' heart rates were consistently in the target zone during the mile run, the rates consistently fell short during their traditional sport activity days. There was just too much standing around during these sessions.

That understanding set the stage for Lawler's next little epiphany. One pleasant Saturday morning, he drove to Madison to catch up on some paperwork. As he pulled into the school parking lot, he noticed eight kids playing touch football on the school lawn. Four kids were on each side. Lawler sat in his car watching and noticed how every kid in the game seemed to be in perpetual motion.

Then the lightbulb went on for Lawler again.

"Here we are, as professionals, we're creating games of 11-on-11 and we have heart rate monitors telling us the kids aren't active in class, and yet they come out on Saturday morning playing 4-on-4 and they're very active," said Lawler.

He drove home that Saturday thinking that he and his colleagues needed to change the way they used sports in their PE curriculum. On Monday, Lawler took his insight to Crackel and Vermaat, suggesting that the department needed to switch from full-sided games to small-sided games in order to get students more active. Crackel and Vermaat were quick to agree.

"Of all the things we've done in our PE program, small-sided games is one of the most important aspects in this evolution of change," said Lawler.

"Number one, it didn't cost us any money. Number two, the heart rate monitors told us that with small-sided games every kid in class was active and their heart rates were elevated enough to derive fitness benefits. In 4-on-4, it's pretty hard to hide."

It wasn't just 4-on-4 football. Madison's small-sided games included 3-on-3 basketball, 3-on-3 soccer, and modified small-sided softball games. Fitness levels improved at a higher rate than during the full-sided games. Interestingly, sport skills were improving as well.

"We found that not only did the nonathletes' fitness levels improve but so did their sports skills. In addition, their interest and enjoyment of team sports increased as well," said Lawler. "The move to small-sided games was a win from every perspective. I think a big reason is that in small-sided games, the nonathletic kids couldn't be ostracized to the degree they were before. They were involved."

Vermaat believes that the department's commitment to innovation—of which the switch to small-sided games is only one example—accelerated the evolution from "Old PE" to "New PE."

"With small-sided teams, we moved from 8 fields of kids playing to 20 fields of kids playing," says Vermaat. "In addition to utilizing small-sided teams to get kids more active, we added elements that allowed kids to quickly solve arguments—like rock, paper, scissors—and get back to playing and moving."

At this point, the Madison PE staff began to use the acronym FITS for their sport segments: Fitness Integrated Through Sports. With the FITS approach, the number one objective was no longer mastery of sport skills but getting kids moving through sports. It was still a sport model, but it was now a fitness-oriented sport model.

Another unexpected benefit from the FITS approach was that it helped the students improve their leadership, teamwork, and communication skills. With small-sided teams, everyone was needed, and nobody could hide; thus, everyone—athlete and nonathlete—had to pull together, talk to each other, and learn to motivate each other in order to successfully compete in the games. As a result, the athletes in class didn't dominate all aspects of the sport activities anymore.

"One benefit we didn't expect—and that is so hard to measure—is that in small-sided games, all the students were involved," said Lawler. "This had positive consequences. When we used the full-sided teams approach, the athletes were the whole show. The non-athletically-inclined students just stood around and watched. In 4-on-4, you may have one athlete on each team. The athlete looks around and says, 'Well, I'm going to have to use everyone here.' All of a sudden the other three, the nonathletes, are involved and have to play a major role.

"In the Old PE days, we used to talk about things like leadership, communication, and teamwork being important reasons why we played team sports in PE class, but the truth was only the athletes were truly involved and developing those skills," said Lawler. "With small-sided teams, we had a much higher percentage of students developing those skills."

Another benefit of the FITS approach to sports, in combination with the use of heart rate monitors, was that Lawler and his staff could use the heart rate data at the end of each school year to evaluate the small-sided games from a fitness perspective. The heart rate data helped them make adjustments to the curriculum, deemphasizing those sports and other activities with limited fitness benefits.

"We still play sports, though much less than before," concluded Lawler. "We just do them within a fitness model through small-sided sports."

Creating the Madison Health Club

In addition to the weekly mile run, the adoption of heart rate monitors, and the switch from full-sided sports to small-sided sports, Lawler and the Madison PE team began a long-term project: building a full-fledged health club within the walls of Madison Junior High.

Strength training had long been a regular two-week unit at Madison— even in the Old PE days. In an era when many physical education teachers thought weight training wasn't safe for kids in junior high school, Lawler had been a big supporter. He had researched the safety of weight training

Early on, Phil saw the value of creating a health club for all students to access at Madison Junior High.

for young people ages 12 to 15 and came away convinced that it was safe as long as lighter weights and higher repetitions were used.

With their move to a fitness model, the Madison PE team put an increased emphasis on building their "health club," especially by adding cardiovascular equipment. Lawler found himself going to garage sales on weekends looking for good deals on treadmills, stationary bikes, and other exercise equipment that he could add to the Madison Health Club.

"I became so convinced that we needed to build a true health club at Madison, with strength and cardiovascular equipment, that I found myself looking at garage sale ads in the paper in search of good deals for equipment, much to my wife's chagrin sometimes," said Lawler laughing.

In fact, on more than a few Monday mornings in the early '90s, Lawler could be seen hauling an exercise bike or two into Madison Junior High, a prize catch from that weekend's garage sale hunt. Some pieces he bought with his own money, and others he purchased after begging Virgo to somehow find the money in the school budget.

"There were many Mondays when Phil would be at my office door asking me about money for a new piece of exercise equipment," says Virgo. "I remember one time in particular that Phil showed up on a Monday before all the other teachers arrived and told me that he *really* needed $150 for this great piece of exercise equipment and a truck to pick it up. That's how they built their fitness center in the early days, piece by piece."

Lana Bassetto, a former language arts teacher at Madison Junior High in the early years when Lawler was building his PE program, said that Lawler was never discouraged by budget limitations.

"Every time I turned around, Phil had more weights in the weight room, more bikes, etc.," said Bassetto. "He would buy stuff at garage sales, moving sales, wherever he could find a good deal. Most of the time he used his own money. The school budget never stopped him.

"He was doing all this out of love. People could sense that and feel it. On top of that, he has a great personality. He's fun, always happy, upbeat, positive. That attitude alone makes people gravitate toward him and want to help him. He has a contagious spirit.

"After I got out of teaching, I became an aerobics, yoga, and Pilates instructor. Phil knew that and was always sending me or calling me with tips and little factoids about fitness. That's just the kind of person he is."

Throughout Lawler's Old PE years, the centerpiece of Madison's strength-training unit was an old, beat-up, eight-station universal gym machine that the department purchased at a fire-sale price from a local health club that had closed. When it was time for the strength-training unit, they would pull the universal gym machine out of storage, add a few other stations, and presto, a mini–health club. However, Lawler and his colleagues thought the move from a sport model to a fitness model required a significant upgrade.

"Once we made the shift to a health-and-wellness-based fitness model, we decided we needed to develop a full-fledged fitness center with cardio and strength equipment," said Lawler. "We went shopping everywhere we could think of in search of deeply discounted strength and cardio equipment. Finally, we found a company in Chicago that was selling a new line of strength equipment and was willing to give us a bargain closeout price on their old floor equipment. Overnight we had a dream fitness center with enough stations for each student."

The Madison PE uniforms began to reflect the department's focus on health and wellness. The front of the shirt had the slogan "Get Fit for Life at Madison Health Club." One sleeve said, "Warning: An Inactive Lifestyle Could Be Detrimental to Your Health."

Lawler's new fitness-based curriculum now required students to not only run a mile once a week but also complete the health club's strength and cardiovascular stations once a week. Along with the regular use of heart rate monitors and the FITS approach to sports, Madison's fitness-based New PE program was improving annually.

With Madison committed to the New PE approach, Lawler turned his attention to getting Naperville Central High School on board the fitness-based PE bandwagon. Central was the next stop for Madison Junior High's students, and Lawler wanted the fitness momentum they'd gained through three years of Madison's New PE program to continue during their high school years.

Lawler's Next Challenge: Converting Mr. Z

Phil Lawler and Paul Zientarski had been friends for years. In the early years of New PE at Madison, Lawler was also the district physical education coordinator for Naperville School District 203. As such, he would occasionally leave his home base at Madison and visit the district's other physical education instructors. Zientarski was the physical education department chair at Naperville Central High School and as such was Lawler's first target.

It was during these semiformal PE discussions that Lawler and Zientarski (known to almost everyone at Naperville Central High as Mr. Z) cultivated a strong friendship and eventually a working relationship built around the New PE.

But converting Zientarski to the New PE wouldn't come easy. Like Lawler, Mr. Z was viewed by others as a coach first, teacher second. Zientarski started his career with the intention of being a physical education teacher first and foremost. However, early in his career, he got caught up in the "addiction of coaching" as he terms it. Coaching began to define his career path.

"Early on, I took new jobs based on my coaching prowess, not my teaching," says Zientarski. While Lawler concentrated on coaching baseball, Zientarski coached football, soccer, track, and cross country.

Zientarski was slow to come around to Lawler's New PE sales pitch. Nevertheless, Lawler relentlessly pestered Zientarski to get some heart rate monitors and start using them to help transition from a sport focus to a fitness focus in PE classes.

"I kept telling Z, 'Man you've got to try these heart rate monitors. It's unbelievable what kind of information you can get,'" said Lawler. "But Z kept putting me off."

In fact, Zientarski grew tired of Lawler's New PE evangelism. He didn't think radical change was necessary—or practical.

"I said, 'Phil, my god, these are $250 apiece,'" said Zientarski, referring to the heart rate monitors Lawler was promoting. "'If I even buy five of them, that's the bulk of my year's budget. I won't have enough money left for balls and bats.' Well, he kept bugging me and kept bugging me. So, I finally relented and bought one heart rate monitor that would download and five that didn't. They weren't as sophisticated. In our first year of using them, we found a few kids with heart problems. Mitral valve prolapse in one student was the biggest one we found."

That was all Zientarski needed. He was sold. He no longer needed Lawler to inspire him. In fact, he soon became part of Lawler's growing army and a fellow advocate for heart rate monitors and what they could do for kids.

"Paul can be quite stubborn sometimes, but once he buys into something, he's a real bulldog," said Lawler.

"In addition to the health aspects and finding the heart problems, the heart rate monitor taught me—for the first time—that I could treat kids as individuals," said Zientarski. "Now we could tell kids they could get an *A* for staying in the target heart rate zone. From the most athletic to the most nonathletic, every kid had an opportunity to get an *A* based on effort and staying in the zone. We actually told some kids that were walking the mile to slow down and stay in the zone.

"I said this is too good. I have to get a classroom set. So, I figured out some ways to the needed funding. I got some parents involved to help raise money, and I ended up having a classroom set of heart rate monitors for the next year, and we've never looked back."

As Zientarski was exploring creative ways to find money for heart rate monitors, he was simultaneously working the traditional school budget route by hounding the school district's technology department to buy heart rate monitors for his department. Finally, the technology team agreed and told Zientarski that there was money in the budget for heart rate monitors.

"Great," said Zientarski. "I don't want them. I want a TriFIT machine instead."

By this time, Zientarski and Lawler both had a nice set of heart rate monitors. They didn't really need any more heart rate monitors. However, Lawler had discovered a company called HealthFirst that made a computerized fitness testing system called TriFIT. The TriFIT machine would allow Zientarski to take the next step in developing personalized wellness plans for kids.

The technology department relented and told Zientarski that he could get a TriFIT machine. The conditions were that if he got the TriFIT machine, he couldn't get any heart rate monitors. Zientarski quickly agreed.

The TriFIT machines allowed Zientarski and Lawler to compare their students with others of the same sex and age on parameters such as body weight, body fat, heart rate, blood pressure, flexibility, strength, cardiovascular conditioning, and so on.

In essence, TriFIT helped them customize physical education for their students. For example, the TriFIT evaluation helped Zientarski, Lawler, and their colleagues create personalized workout plans for each student. Plans included aerobic, strength, and flexibility training as well as sports and other physical activities for each student based on his or her preferences.

With Zientarski on board, Lawler continued to push the envelope with his New PE philosophy and program. He knew he needed to get those with influence and power on his side. Early on he got Virgo, his principal at Madison, to buy in. Then he started focusing on his local school board.

Tim Costello was a long-time school board member for Naperville School District 203 during the years that Lawler's New PE program was evolving. He recalls some of Phil's forays with school board members during board meetings.

"Phil was a passionate advocate for PE in front of the school board," says Costello. "He was totally flipping the PE model upside down with kids, and he wanted to make sure the school board knew why. He would come in and show the board the innovative things he and his colleagues were doing and all the benefits the students were receiving. Phil knew he had to do some politicking in order for his vision to become a reality and continue to grow.

"He had his detractors on the board for a while, but he ended up being well respected by the entire board. He wanted to get to the point where the board thought of PE in the same positive light as they did the Naperville math, science, and language arts programs—if not better."

Word began to spread about the innovative things Lawler and Zientarski were doing with their PE programs in Naperville. Lawler was selling the New PE every chance he got. Eventually, the Madison and Naperville Central PE programs were discovered by a few local news organizations. The focus of the news reports was the programs' fitness orientation—especially the use of heart rate monitors—as well as some of the student health problems that the New PE approach helped catch. Before long, Chicago newspapers and television stations had picked up on the Naperville PE stories.

Lawler became the natural spokesperson for the Naperville School District 203 physical education program. He was a journalist's dream because of his passion, his knowledge, his ease in front of a microphone and camera, and his ability to tell stories that delivered key messages in memorable sound bites.

"He works to get the word out, to get more people on board, to get media attention in order to try and make a difference and make changes more globally rather than just in one or two local locations," said Scott Wikgren, director of the health, physical education, recreation and dance division of Human Kinetics, a leading physical education and sports publisher. "I think he thinks of himself as a 'born-again physical educator.' He realized that the way we were brought up and taught to teach PE left out too many kids. He felt it was a wrong that needed to be made right."

It wasn't long before the national media picked up on Lawler and the revolutionary New PE program in Naperville, Illinois. Articles in *Time, USA Today,* and other major publications highlighted Naperville's health-and-wellness-based physical education programs and the results they were getting.

It was one such article that caught the eye of the new chief executive of a young nonprofit called PE4life.

PE4life Comes to Town

Anne Flannery was getting bleary-eyed going through the stacks of folders on her desk. She had just moved to Washington, DC to start her new position as president and CEO of PE4life, a new nonprofit with a mission to increase the number of quality daily physical education programs for K-12 students.

The former Spalding executive was doing some research on the state of physical education in her still barren PE4life office when she came across a 2000 article in *USA Today* about the "New PE." The article was the cover story in the sports section. Phil Lawler and the Naperville program were featured in the article.

"There were 8 or 10 people quoted in the article from different PE programs around the country, but Phil's quotes really struck me because they fit my own philosophy of what needed to happen with PE—that it needed to embrace health and wellness," recalls Flannery.

Flannery began an ongoing conversation with Lawler about his philosophy and program and about what PE4life's objective was. She spoke with Jim Baugh, PE4life's founder and chairman, about Lawler and what was going on in Naperville. Baugh had also recently become aware of Lawler and his program. He decided to take a look at Lawler's program in person. Baugh came back impressed. He liked the program's focus on health and wellness, especially Lawler's use of heart rate monitors.

"Phil epitomized the entrepreneurial, creative leader I wanted PE4life to be associated with," said Baugh. "Phil's not afraid to buck the system, and he's a very good speaker. Most importantly, he produced results. He was a doer. A lot of people are good at delivering a message but don't deliver.

Phil delivers. He also had passion. Passion is something you can't teach. It was clear his passion was infectious and others wanted to follow him."

Flannery also became increasingly impressed with Lawler.

"My ongoing conversations with Phil confirmed that these guys had an innovative program," said Flannery. "They were focused on health and wellness and not focused on the old dodgeball model of PE. I was intrigued about the possibility of teaming up with Phil's program in some way down the road."

Flannery knew she needed a way to put PE4life on the map. She needed to showcase the PE4life philosophy—quality physical education for all children. She and Baugh thought that Lawler and Naperville 203 were exactly in line with the PE4life approach. They believed that Naperville 203 had an exemplary program that epitomized how PE should look across the country and throughout the world.

While her discussions with Lawler continued, Flannery also began working with a public relations firm on strategies to get physical education in the national consciousness as part of the solution to some of the health ills plaguing the country, including childhood obesity. She eventually got PE4life involved in a press conference promoting physical activity for Americans. This press conference was held before the second presidential debate between Al Gore and George W. Bush in 2000.

Flannery thought she needed a passionate physical education teacher for the press conference and invited Lawler to Washington, DC for the event.

"Phil flew in. We did the press conference in early October in DC at the Willard Hotel," says Flannery. "Phil was eloquent. He told stories that were real about real students. He was terrific."

Lawler soon became PE4life's unofficial spokesperson. When Flannery got questions from reporters, she would often send them Phil's way.

PE4LIFE CORE PRINCIPLES

Over time and with the collaboration of additional exemplary programs and model sites, the PE4life philosophy evolved into the following approach to quality physical education:

- Offer a variety of fitness, sport, leisure, and adventure activities to all students.
- Implement a K-12 standards-based curriculum.
- Provide a safe and encouraging learning environment.
- Use individual assessments.
- Incorporate current technology.
- Extend PE beyond the walls of the gymnasium.
- Ideally, offer PE activities to every child every day.

"Nobody can speak more eloquently and passionately about the important role of PE than Phil," said Flannery. "He's especially good at helping people understand the changes involved in going from the Old PE model to the New PE model."

Flannery began to sense that PE4life needed to formalize the relationship with Lawler and the Naperville 203 School District. She thought Lawler and his PE program in Naperville made PE4life's philosophy tangible. She also admired Lawler's ability to bring the New PE approach to life for all the key target audiences: teachers, school administrators, school board members, parents, and community members.

"I told Phil, 'We've got to find a way to institutionalize this partnership,'" said Flannery. "'We've got to find a way to maximize this.'"

"Anne kept talking about 'institutionalizing this,'" said Lawler. "I kept agreeing with her, but I wasn't sure what she really had in mind or how to go about it. So, I eventually just hooked her up with our administrators."

Within a couple months, Flannery was in Naperville negotiating with Ron Gibson, Naperville 203's assistant superintendent, about establishing a PE4life Institute (which would later become a PE4life Academy Training Center) within the school district. The institute would train teachers from around the country in the "PE4life way." The two sides quickly struck a deal.

"We underwrote half of Phil's teaching load so he could head up our institute in Naperville," said Flannery.

The institute would be designed to "train the trainers." The idea was to get physical education teachers from around the country to visit Naperville for a couple days; train with Lawler, Zientarski, and others; and return home with a blueprint for implementing a health-and-wellness-based PE4life program in their community.

"The whole concept for the institute came from my respect for Pat Summitt, Tennessee's women's basketball coach," said Flannery. "What's always impressed me about Pat is that she's got tons of former players who are now head coaches and successful head coaches. To me that says she's doing it right because she's training the trainers. She's teaching her players during their stay at Tennessee how to be excellent and successful coaches. That was where the whole idea for the first PE4life Institute in Naperville came from."

Flannery had a one-page contract written up for Naperville School District 203. Gibson and Don Weber, the district superintendent, said, "Let's try it," and the PE4life Institute in Naperville, Illinois, was off the ground.

Flannery was hopeful that the PE4life Institute would address what she saw as the three key problems with physical education in the country: (1) the dramatic decline in the number of students taking physical education classes on a daily basis; (2) the continued emphasis on the "sport model" of physical education that overemphasizes participation in team sports (and the development of skills for those sports) at the expense of physical fitness, health, and wellness education; and (3) the assignment of grades to students based on skills and innate abilities versus effort and progress toward individual goals.

Initially, the PE4life Institute focused on training PE teachers. However, it gradually became clear that training PE teachers alone wasn't that effective. The PE teachers would leave Naperville fired up, but they would get back to their school and run into roadblocks with fellow teachers, administrators, school board members, parents, and so on. So, PE4life changed their requirements for attendance. Schools would now be required to bring a well-rounded team representing the school, the school district, and the local community to the PE4life Institute for training. These teams included not only PE teachers, but also a variety of other key influencers, including administrators, school board members, community leaders, influential parents, and occasionally even a member of the local media.

An increasing number of teams from schools and communities around the country began visiting the PE4life Institute in Naperville—which in addition to Lawler's Madison Junior High program also included Zientarski's program at Naperville Central High School and Todd Keating's program at River Wood Elementary—to receive the training necessary to transform their PE programs from being focused on sport skills to being focused on health and wellness.

Institute attendees learned about the "PE4life way," which at its essence is about getting kids active now and instilling the lifetime benefits of health and wellness. It's about enabling each student to maintain a physically active lifestyle forever. The training emphasizes fitness and well-being, not athleticism. It eliminates practices that humiliate students such as dodgeball. And it stresses assessing students on effort and their progress in reaching personal goals related to physical activity and fitness. In essence, the PE4life way is about exposing kids to the fun and long-term benefits of movement—on a daily basis.

"If children take away one thing from their PE4life experience, it should be the importance of daily exercise," says Anne Flannery. "Daily physical education is crucial in helping children reap the long-term benefits of physical fitness and establishing this healthy habit for life."

Baugh echoes that belief.

"Physical education is the most effective grassroots program available to get children active today and help them establish healthy fitness habits that will last a lifetime," maintains Baugh.

"Becoming a PE4life Institute brought more notoriety to our program," said Lawler. "It enhanced our credibility and helped put a national—and even international—spotlight on our program. And it gave PE4life a tangible example of their philosophy. It was a win–win arrangement."

Since its inception, the PE4life Institute (now called the PE4life Academy Training Centers and model sites) has hosted attendees from 42 states (see figure 2.1) and 10 foreign countries, teaching them about the New PE and how to implement it.

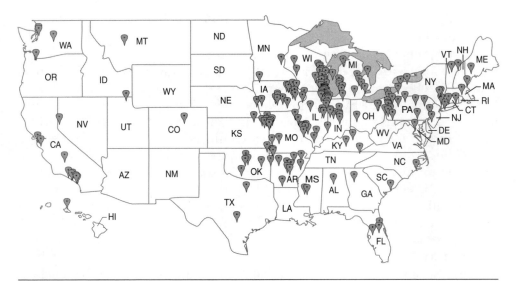

Figure 2.1　PE4life impact in the United States.

The establishment of the PE4life Institute gave Lawler a bigger pulpit from which to spread his message about the New PE. He was now a half-time teacher and half-time evangelist for the benefits of quality physical education.

In Lawler, PE4life secured a passionate, respected spokesperson for their cause. As the partnership between Naperville 203 and PE4life evolved, Lawler's exposure in the media increased, and his PE4life messages began to reach a much wider audience.

Another positive development from the partnership was that PE4life in general, and Phil Lawler in particular, played a major role in the development of the successful Physical Education for Progress (PEP) federal grant program. The PEP grant program was passed by Congress in 2001 to provide schools with grants to upgrade their PE programs in light of the rise in childhood obesity and declining PE budgets.

Lawler spent hours on the phone with Carol White (Alaska Senator Ted Stevens' chief of staff) working on the language and specifics of the PEP program. Stevens became the program's primary sponsor in large part because of White's urging. Lawler developed a strong working relationship with White, who had a lot of influence with Senator Stevens. Over time, Lawler and White would grow to become good friends. Eventually, White, with a lot of input from Lawler, would end up writing the language for the PEP grant program, which to date has awarded nearly $500 million in federal grants for schools through the Carol M. White Physical Education Program.

After the partnership with Naperville to be the flagship PE4life Institute was formalized, others soon followed, demonstrating quality PE in diverse geographical and SES situations—small town Titusville, Pennsylvania; rural Grundy Center, Iowa; inner city Indianapolis, Indiana; booming suburb Rogers, Arkansas; and urban core Kansas City, Missouri.

Overcoming Hurdles to Keep the Momentum Going

Even with the credibility and exposure that PE4life brought, Lawler still faced many hurdles in his quest to transform physical education—even within his own district. Several teachers and administrators in the Naperville 203 school district didn't see the value of physical education in the school setting, and they wanted to scale back its role, not watch it grow and become more prominent.

"At times, the fight for quality physical education in Naperville 203 got a little ugly," said Lawler. "There was a period where we were battling a lady in the curriculum office—whose name I'd rather not mention—on a regular basis. She was turned off by PE, and the last thing she wanted to see was for PE to gain more credibility and grow in her school district."

Lawler also dealt with jealousy among a few of his PE colleagues across the district.

"When we started to find creative ways to get nice equipment that nobody else had, some PE teachers at other schools in the district would ask 'Why is Madison getting all the equipment?'" recalled Lawler. "Also, at other times, some teachers would be jealous and upset that the media always wanted to come to Madison for their stories.

"At other times, people would be jealous that schools and communities from around the country—and eventually around the world—were coming to Madison and Central for PE4life training and not to their particular school," said Lawler. "I just looked at the jealousy as a minor nuisance to deal with and certainly didn't let it hinder what we needed to do to keep our program and the movement going forward.

"Ironically, when the school district started purchasing some of the new PE technology for physical education programs across the entire school district—like heart rate monitors and TriFIT machines—some PE teachers didn't want it! I guess they thought it was too big of a change or too much work."

Perhaps one of Lawler's biggest challenges came in the form of a Naperville parent who just happened to also be an Illinois State Representative. Her name was Mary Lou Cowlishaw.

"Mary Lou Cowlishaw hated PE," said Lawler. "She saw no value in it. I think she might have set the record for most excused absences from PE for her daughter!

"When Illinois' daily physical education mandate would come up in the Illinois legislature, she would vote against it every time. Well, a few PE colleagues and myself made it our mission to change her mind. We called her. We presented in front of her. We sent her all the new research touting the benefits of health-and-wellness-based PE.

"Finally, she came around and saw the light. She ultimately became one of our greatest supporters. I still remember the day she told me 'Phil, you have completely changed my mind on PE.' She even came to one of our PE4life press conferences and waived two PE4life brochures at the media, educators, and parents in attendance and said, 'We need more of this!'

"We didn't turn around all of our opponents, but we eventually got to a lot of them."

Lawler rarely showed frustration with his antagonists. He focused on understanding their points and patiently building an argument to overcome them.

"There were definitely hurdles, but I just looked at it as a challenge and part of the change process," said Lawler.

"Phil Lawler has always been somebody that wasn't going to stand for the status quo," said Rick Schupbach, the PE4life Academy director in Grundy Center, Iowa. "He's willing to be on the cutting edge of change. And I always say that when you're on the cutting edge you're really on the bleeding edge because you're going to take some shots. Lawler had the willingness to carve out a new path."

> Phil Lawler has always been somebody that wasn't going to stand for the status quo. He had the willingness to carve out a new path.

Here's another challenge that Lawler and PE4life had early on: Although physical education teachers would leave their training in Naperville educated and enthused, they would report that they were struggling to develop and implement a PE4life program in their schools. In addition to getting administrators, school board members, and others to join the PE teachers at the PE4life Academy Training Center, Lawler and his PE4life colleagues realized that they needed to arm their academy graduates with more tools.

"After we had worked with Phil and with the Naperville 203 School District for a while, we realized that teachers could come in and view this model program in action and get excited," says Brenda VanLengen, a member of PE4life's board of directors. "Then when it came time for them to go home, they didn't have the tools they needed to actually get things started at their own schools. They were inspired and were impressed, but they were overwhelmed in some ways. They didn't have what they needed to go back home and make changes in their own programs.

"That's when we knew we needed to develop some educational materials—especially a training manual—to help schools around the country develop their own programs, while incorporating PE4life principles. When we made that decision, there was a sense of urgency for us.

"I called Phil, and on a New Year's Eve afternoon, I flew to Chicago and we spent the entire day at a hotel next to the Chicago O'Hare airport. Phil talked and I typed. I had already heard his presentation over and over, but I wanted to really try to capture some of his stories, examples, and his explanations on how to make changes within the school setting. That New Year's Eve afternoon, in a Chicago airport hotel, was the beginning of our PE4life Training Manual.

"I also went to others like Tim McCord, Rick Schupbach, Beth Kirkpatrick, and others that had experienced a PE4life training session. But it was that New Year's Eve day that I spent with Phil that really got the training manual started. That's always going to be a special memory for me—Phil's willingness to do that, to make that effort on New Year's Eve, to sit down and share stories for hours on end while I furiously typed away . . . That's a special memory I have of Phil's passion and dedication to the cause."

◇ ◇ ◇ ◇ ◇ ◇ ◇ ◇ ◇ ◇ ◇ ◇

Today, the state of PE in Naperville 203 is excellent, and detractors are very difficult to find. In fact, the Madison Junior High physical education program has been selected multiple times as the best curriculum in the school by both parents and students.

"When our seniors graduate today, they're given a 25-page report that outlines their progress in physical education from 4th to 12th grade," said Lawler. "It lists fitness scores, medical screenings like EKGs, cholesterol screenings, blood pressure, etc. It has a nutrition section and a family history section. It gives them a status report on their fitness levels as they graduate and goals moving forward.

"This is very important and can serve them the rest of their lives. Our diseases are 70 percent lifestyle and 30 percent genetic. Their Naperville PE4life experience, captured in this report, can serve them the rest of their lives through a healthier lifestyle."

"Former students come back all the time and tell me they're grateful for our New PE program," says Zientarski. "I recently had a former student call me and tell me that her roommate sits in their college dorm room while she goes to exercise at the recreation center all the time. She says her roommate drinks Mountain Dew while she drinks water. She thanked me for the wellness education she got. She didn't want to put on the 'freshman 15 (pounds)' and was glad she had the education to know how to avoid it. Those types of stories happen all the time."

chapter

3

THE QUEST FOR HEALTHIER STUDENTS

> **"I** wish physical education was taught across the nation like it is taught in Naperville, Illinois. You will end up saving more lives through your profession as a physical education instructor than I will ever be able to as a physician. Please make physical education teachers throughout the country aware of the immense effects their efforts can have in developing a healthier population."
>
> —Dr. Michael Kretz, a 25-year practicing physician, in a note to Phil Lawler

Phil Lawler sat at his kitchen table eating breakfast on a cold morning in 1993 and couldn't believe what he was reading in the morning's *Naperville Sun*. Dr. Vincent Buffalino, a renowned Naperville cardiologist, had recently completed a cholesterol screening study at Westmont High School, a nearby school. Buffalino discovered that 42 percent of the students had high cholesterol. The story noted that Buffalino was one of the first doctors in the country to study the cholesterol levels of children ages 10 to 18.

Lawler made a note to try to contact Buffalino as soon as possible. He finished his breakfast and headed to Madison to share his latest finding with his PE colleagues.

"This guy cares about the health of our young people," said Lawler at that morning's PE staff meeting. "Plus, he's right in our backyard. We have to let him know about our program and see if we can get him involved. It would greatly enhance our credibility."

As his PE program continued to grow and gain acceptance, Lawler's eyes were getting bigger. He wanted to take the New PE message beyond the limited physical education field. His instincts told him that he had to get the health care world involved. If the new wellness-based PE philosophy at Madison and Naperville Central was going to be optimally effective, Lawler needed to reach out to top medical doctors and get their endorsement and involvement.

Lawler spent the next few days thinking about how best to approach Buffalino. He was confident that Buffalino would be a powerful ally for his fledgling wellness-based PE program. But what was the first step? How could he get Buffalino interested and involved? Would he have the time?

"The article about Dr. Buffalino and his cholesterol testing program convinced me he was our man, but I didn't know how to approach him," recalled Lawler.

Then an idea hit him. The DuPage County Physical Education Institute was coming up. Who would make a better keynote speaker than Dr. Vincent Buffalino?

The following day, Lawler went to Buffalino's office at Naperville's Edward Hospital—without an appointment—to try to get a few minutes with Buffalino. Lawler's mission was to tell the cardiologist about some of the innovative things he was doing in his PE program and to explore the possibility of Buffalino speaking at the upcoming PE conference.

Lawler considered calling Buffalino with the invitation but thought he would have a better chance of getting him to agree to speak at the conference if he asked him face-to-face. As anyone who knew him can attest, Lawler's passion, while palpable on the phone, was conveyed even more effectively in person.

As Lawler sat in his waiting area, Buffalino was curious about why a PE teacher—who wasn't his patient—would want to talk to him. So, to satisfy his curiosity, he decided to take a few minutes out of his packed schedule to chat with Lawler.

"The first time I met Phil was when he came in to pitch his physical education conference," says Buffalino while reflecting on that first meeting with Lawler more than 15 years ago. "He talked about my cholesterol testing with kids and his new fitness and health PE program. Almost immediately I was struck by his passion and agreed to speak at his conference."

Buffalino had never thought about physical education teachers as possible allies in his fight against rising cholesterol levels in young people, but he was encouraged after learning the details of Lawler's wellness-based program. He also thought that Lawler oozed sincerity about his desire to use PE to improve cardiovascular health in young people.

"I went to the conference, and I told all these PE teachers that we need to start doing something about high cholesterol early," said Buffalino.

"We need to start educating kids in elementary school and junior high about lifestyle choices instead of waiting until they're 35 to 40 years old. I stressed that I was much more interested in preventing heart disease than treating it."

Lawler was fired up after the conference. He thought that his commitment to the New PE had been validated by Buffalino.

"Listening to Buffalino reinforced my belief in wellness-based PE and spurred me to commit even more to heart rate monitors, other forms of technology, and medical evaluations like cholesterol testing," said Lawler.

As much as Lawler was energized by the work of Buffalino, Buffalino was equally inspired by what he saw Lawler, Zientarski, and their colleagues teaching in Naperville 203 physical education classes.

"They were doing great things. I thought it was especially important that they were using measurement and evaluation as part of their programs. We need science to measure these kids in order to know how much we need to push them and how much to pull back," said Buffalino. "Heart rate monitors are perfect for this so-called New PE. It's really exercise for life combined with sensible nutrition. But measurement is important to know where the kids are along the way."

Ironically, the positive reaction Buffalino received from Lawler, Zientarski, and others at the DuPage PE conference was in stark contrast to the reaction he received from fellow medical doctors in the community after the publication of the news story about his cholesterol study with children.

"A couple pediatricians in town were quoted in a follow-up article in the paper saying I was trying to take ice cream away from kids and unnecessarily scaring mothers," says Buffalino. "I don't think I was unnecessarily scaring mothers at all. It's very clear that kids with cholesterol problems continue into adulthood in a high percentage of cases. It's easier to educate and change behavior in junior high than it is with 35- to 40-year-olds. We recently had six guys between 28 and 30 years old in this hospital with heart attacks in a 30-day period. Junior high school certainly isn't too young to be concerned about cholesterol."

Buffalino, who remains one of Naperville's top cardiologists today, says he was as surprised as anyone else about the findings from his groundbreaking research.

"I was so shocked with our initial findings of 40 percent of kids with high cholesterol that I thought we'd done something wrong," says Buffalino while leaning back in a leather desk chair in his spacious office at Edward Hospital. "We did the tests again to make sure we were right the first time. We were."

After the disconcerting cholesterol readings from Westmont, Buffalino launched the DuPage County Heart Study. This study took the testing he did at Westmont to schools across the county.

"We used finger prick tests so there was no blood to draw or anything," said Buffalino. "It was pretty straightforward and easy."

This time Buffalino and his colleagues tested 4,000 kids within the county. The results showed that 35 percent of the students had high cholesterol readings.

Upset by the research findings and energized by Lawler, Buffalino agreed to form an alliance with the PE programs in Naperville 203. Lawler believed that the relationship with Buffalino brought instant credibility to his physical education program and its new fitness-oriented model. With Buffalino involved and providing an endorsement of Lawler's efforts, fellow teachers, administrators, board members, and parents began to take notice and accept Lawler's New PE program.

"I have always felt physical education teachers are the Rodney Dangerfields of education—'absolutely no respect,'" said Lawler. "So, I figured I needed the voice of a medical doctor to help convince the community of the value of a quality, wellness-based physical education program. Once I saw the success of working with Buffalino, I wanted to expand our link to the medical community, and out of that came our medical advisory board for the school district.

"This board has developed into a great tool for improving communication and improving children's health in our community. Early, we had a difficult time convincing medical people with busy schedules to commit to serving on this committee. The first year there were only a few doctors interested. Seven years later, we had more than 40 doctors meeting for over two hours. Besides doctors, we included school nurses, athletic trainers, social workers, etc."

Buffalino's perception of physical education—and its potential for enhancing health—has grown immensely through the years because of his partnership with Lawler and Naperville 203's physical education programs.

"Physical education teachers can make a difference," said Buffalino. "Phil's career epitomizes this. On a certain level, he's just a local PE teacher. On another level, he's so much more. This guy started where he was and created a movement. First, he changed the thinking of a school, and then a school district, and then a community—exercise is now part of the culture of the whole community of Naperville. Then he started a movement across the country and even internationally. He's a true game changer."

Today, the relationship between the Naperville 203 physical education program and the local medical community has evolved to the point where, in addition to the annual cholesterol screening tests, every kid in the school district gets EKGs.

"Since the inception of the EKG program, more than 25 kids have been detected with heart rhythm disturbances—things that lead to unexpected death in youth," says Buffalino. "We have a voluntary workforce of 1,500 parents that do the EKGs. It's the largest screening program in the country."

"Phil is an idea man," said Virgo. "I don't know of any educator who thinks more progressively than Phil."

That would be proven over and over again.

Lawler was thrilled with how his relationship with Dr. Buffalino had evolved and how it led to the formation of the school district's medical advisory board. The success he experienced with Buffalino and other local physicians emboldened him. His next target was much bigger: Dr. Kenneth Cooper, the world-renowned "Father of Aerobics" and head of the Cooper Aerobics Center in Dallas, Texas.

Cooper started the aerobics craze in 1968 with the publication of his book *Aerobics*. Soon after, he founded the Cooper Aerobics Center, a health and wellness facility with a cornerstone of preventive measures such as physical activity, nutrition, and stress management.

"Our focus in our transformed PE program was cardiovascular fitness," said Lawler. "I figured there wasn't anyone better than the 'Father of Aerobics' to learn from and maybe to get involved in our program in some way."

After a couple calls to the Cooper Aerobics Center, Lawler was able to talk to Todd Whitthorne, a close colleague of Cooper's (and today the president and CEO of Cooper Concepts, a subsidiary under the Cooper umbrella). Whitthorne was immediately impressed with Lawler's enthusiasm and evangelism for his physical education program.

"When I first spoke with Phil, I was quickly struck by his energy and his will to make a difference," said Whitthorne. "He is relentless in terms of spreading this message about what physical education can be."

After speaking with Lawler a few more times, Whitthorne thought the passionate PE teacher from Naperville, Illinois, would make a great guest on Dr. Cooper's nationally syndicated radio show, *Healthy Living*. He told Cooper about Lawler and set up a phone meeting for the two.

"He's an impressive guy," said Cooper about his first conversation with Lawler. "And his passion is quickly infectious."

Cooper told Whitthorne to go ahead and book Lawler for an upcoming *Healthy Living* show.

Lawler was a popular guest on *Healthy Living* and was asked back several times by Cooper. The show's audience was always inspired by Lawler's passion and the description of his PE program—and how different that program was from the gym class they remembered from their youth.

"He's amazing," said Cooper. "I think he's the ultimate PE instructor."

As Lawler's relationship with Cooper grew stronger, Lawler thought he'd take the next bold step and ask Cooper to speak at his DuPage County PE Institute in Naperville.

"I asked him to come to Illinois to speak at our conference, thinking the chances weren't great that a famous and busy doctor—who speaks all over the world at major medical conferences—would agree to come to our conference of elementary, middle school, and high school PE teachers," said Lawler. "It turned out that he agreed fairly easily. He was intrigued enough by our conversations to want to take a firsthand look at what we were doing in Naperville."

Not surprisingly, Cooper was a big hit at Lawler's PE conference that year. And like Buffalino before him, Cooper was impressed with Lawler and Zientarski and their programs at Madison Junior High and Naperville Central High, respectively.

"The first time I saw the Naperville operation, I thought it was clever and unique," says Cooper. "It was a new concept, scientifically based, looking at outcomes. I saw the leadership of Phil Lawler and Paul Zientarski. I thought it was a program that probably set an example for PE programs in schools nationwide, if not worldwide."

Cooper was also impressed by the fact that all Naperville 203 students, including athletes, take physical education daily—without exception.

"They require all their athletes, who are normally excused from PE in other schools because they participate in sports, to take PE," says Cooper. "That's because they incorporate a lot of health and wellness topics. It's not just sports, like it is at so many schools. It's interesting that since they incorporated mandatory PE for all athletes—about 15 years ago—they've won more championships than they won in the previous 50 years."

Although Cooper had long been active in promoting children's health, his long-term relationship with Lawler caused him to focus even more on

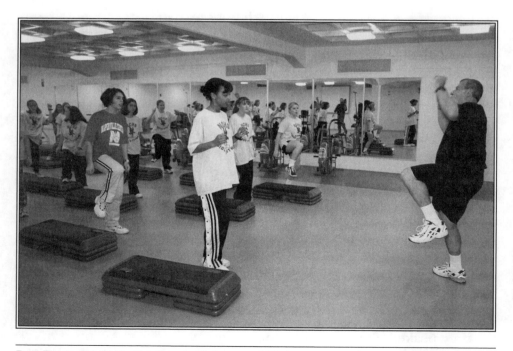

Paul Zientarski, Phil's friend and colleague, quickly became convinced of the benefits and necessity of heart rate monitors.

the importance of children's wellness, and it spurred him to undertake several major initiatives.

"I've used Phil's work and great experience in the field to set up programs we have in Texas that are now getting international interest," says Cooper.

After visiting Naperville, Cooper flew back home and grew increasingly frustrated with the poor levels of health and wellness of K-12 students in Texas.

"Phil helped get me on the warpath for physical education here in Texas," says Cooper. "It hasn't been easy. We've had tremendous rebellion here."

Cooper initiated several wellness efforts in Texas targeting K-12 students, including a multiyear campaign to get physical education back in Texas' schools on a regular basis. It was a long, hard battle, and there's still a long way to go, but Cooper's commitment and hard work—and Lawler's ongoing support—finally resulted in the passage of Texas Senate Bill 530 in 2007.

"Senate Bill 530 brought PE back into the schools on a regular basis for the first time in 20 years in Texas, making it mandatory for grades K-5 and part of six semesters for 6th, 7th, and 8th grades," says Cooper. "We also tested the fitness levels of 2.6 million kids in Texas, through the 12th grade—starting in January 2008—on the Fitnessgram test. I used, as a basis for this fitness research, the example of the programs in Naperville.

"At the Cooper Center, we've been doing things with kids for years, but my interest didn't really peak in working with kids until about five years ago; and Phil Lawler's a big reason for that. I speak very highly of Phil. His example is a big reason I worked so hard to raise $3.1 million in three months so we could equip all 9,000 schools in Texas with the equipment to do the Fitnessgram testing and to prepare 20,000 teachers to do the test."

Besides quantifying that the overall fitness level of Texas' schoolchildren was poor, Cooper's youth fitness study in Texas found that there were significant associations between fitness levels and academic achievement (see the sidebar on p. 38). Fit kids performed better academically. These findings supported the link between fitness and academic performance found in previous studies.

Cooper's admiration for Lawler grew through the years to the point where he considered him a peer and valued colleague.

"I talk about Phil all the time," said Cooper. "I refer to him in many of my presentations. I talk about the great, unique, and creative programs they're conducting there in Naperville and how successful they've been. He's obsessive. He's compassionate. He's a researcher. What he's done in physical education, I've tried to expand to the field of medicine, to the field of preventive medicine. Phil Lawler's very creative. He's a revolutionary.

"Bottom line, I think Phil Lawler is the most important person there is for improving physical education in the world," said Cooper. "I know Phil certainly peaked my interest in targeting kids. We need to focus more on lifestyle management in this country instead of disease management."

"Phil Lawler is legendary," concluded Cooper.

COOPER YOUTH FITNESS STUDY IN TEXAS

Significant associations were consistently found between physical fitness and various indicators of academic achievement, specifically the following:

- **Academic performance** – Higher levels of fitness are associated with better academic performance.
- **School attendance** – Higher levels of fitness are associated with better school attendance.
- **School incidents** – Higher levels of fitness are associated with fewer negative school incidents (i.e., disciplinary issues).

The Cooper Institute, 2009, www.cooperinstitute.org.

The Naperville PE4life program that Buffalino and Cooper rave about has produced some impressive fitness-related outcomes.

For example, results from a Fitnessgram assessment conducted by Naperville School District 203 showed that 97 percent of ninth graders in Naperville 203 scored in the healthy fitness zone. Meanwhile, the same test done on ninth graders in the state of California revealed that only 67 percent of California ninth graders scored in the healthy fitness zone.

"Even more startling, in California, only 49 percent of kids met the healthy standard for cardiovascular conditioning (based on the mile run), while ours were at 80 percent," notes Zientarski, Naperville Central's physical education director.

Fitness levels can improve dramatically when a commitment to fitness-based physical education is made. And that improvement can happen in any community in the country. It doesn't need to be an upper-middle-class suburb like Naperville, Illinois.

PE4life has seen results similar to Naperville's in situations varying from a small farm town (Grundy Center, Iowa) to an economically distressed industrial town (Titusville, Pennsylvania) to an inner-city school (Kansas City, Missouri). Fitness-based physical education programs have been shown to improve the overall health and wellness of the student body no matter what the demographics of a particular school or community may be.

Consider the results achieved in just one year at Woodland Elementary, an urban Kansas City, Missouri, school with a low economic profile.

Woodland fourth and fifth graders showed dramatic improvement across the Fitnessgram's six health and fitness indicators after one year of integrating PE4life Core Principles. Before that, the students at Woodland participated in one 50-minute PE class a week. The school moved to a daily physical education program for 45 minutes per day and also moved from a sport-centric model to a fitness-centric model, including the use of assessment technology such as heart rate monitors. After one year,

Woodland fourth and fifth graders showed dramatic improvement across the Fitnessgram's six health and fitness indicators after one year of integrating PE4life Core Principles.

cardiovascular fitness improved 207 percent, strength levels were up 433 percent, and flexibility improved 182 percent among the school's fourth and fifth graders.

Rick Schupbach—director of the Grundy Center, Iowa, PE4life Academy Training Center—says that a key to success for health-and-wellness-based physical education programs is to measure the impact the program is having. Technological tools, including heart rate monitors and other forms of technological assessment, are the cornerstones of his program.

"Data drives decisions," says Schupbach, repeating his favorite mantra. "We're not going to change the culture of physical education without the data to support our messages with administrators, school board members, community leaders, and parents."

Zientarski agrees with Schupbach but adds that the time spent in PE class, by itself, isn't enough to make the desired short- and long-term changes necessary to significantly improve fitness and overall health levels. He believes that support from the school's staff, parents, and the rest of the community is key. He also says that positive changes are the result of efforts made by the students themselves—in school and outside of class.

"It's not our job to make students fit, but rather to provide them with the information and lead them to an awareness of the value and importance of taking care of themselves," says Zientarski. "We urge individual goal setting. It's more of a fitness club mentality, promoting individualized programs offering students the chance to take themselves as high as they can.

"We strive for an end result of imparting the intrinsic desire to be fit, along with the knowledge of how to accomplish that—something they can carry with them throughout their lives."

Schupbach believes that a major roadblock in getting the buy-in of other teachers, parents, and community leaders is the "Old PE" perception of physical education inside and outside the walls of the school.

"Most adults still look at the physical education program as being a feeder for the district's sports teams," says Schupbach. "I take offense to that. I want to see physical education taken outside the walls of the gym and have it called 'lifestyles education.'"

If the Old PE is commonly seen as a developmental program for a school's sport teams, the New PE is seen as an educational program that teaches healthy living for a lifetime.

According to a 2010 survey from the Physical Activity Council, Americans who didn't have physical education in school are 2.5 times more likely to be sedentary adults. The same survey indicated that children who take PE in school are 3 to 4 times more likely to participate in physical activities outside of school during their school years relative to their peers who don't take PE.

These data are important because they support research that shows that physically active kids are much more likely to be active adults than inactive kids are.

"There's a huge difference between the Old PE and the New PE," said Lawler. "It requires an ongoing education and communications effort targeting students, parents, teachers, administrators, school board members, the medical profession, corporate executives, community leaders, and the media."

As word spread through the media about the cutting-edge PE programs in Naperville and the amazing results they were getting, more and more school districts and communities began making the trek to Naperville to see firsthand what all the excitement was about.

One such community was Owensboro, Kentucky.

In 2000, a children's health assessment in Owensboro revealed a significant increase in obesity and diabetes among the area's children. The assessment drew concern from Owensboro Mercy Health System, the three area school districts, and corporate leaders within the community.

A task force of school and community leaders determined that engaging the community's youth in a program to change lifestyles through awareness and physical fitness was the best way to establish a healthier community. While researching viable solutions to improve physical fitness in the schools and to increase the future health of the area's students, the group from Owensboro discovered the PE4life Academy Training Center in Naperville, Illinois.

A group of school faculty and hospital employees led by Greg Carlson, former CEO of Owensboro Mercy Medical Park, made the trip to Naperville. They were impressed by the state-of-the-art approach to physical education they witnessed.

"As a health care delivery system, we've believed for a long time that no matter how much money we throw at the disease/treatment side of medicine, we would never be able to improve the health of our communities the way a quality physical education program for children would," said Carlson.

Excited by what they saw, the Owensboro coalition returned to Kentucky and began to work on a community plan for a program similar to Naperville's.

Funding was raised through a partnership between the Mercy Health System, several local corporations, and the area school districts. This funding enabled the town of 90,000 to purchase the equipment and training necessary to establish a state-of-the-art physical education program in the six middle schools and two high schools. The cost of restructuring the physical education program was $50,000 to $75,000 per school. All six middle schools and two high schools have integrated PE4life Core Principles, and the upward trend regarding the health assessments of the community's youth is encouraging.

By 2005, stories like Owensboro's—combined with the success of PE4life Academy Training Centers in Naperville, Illinois; Titusville, Pennsylvania; Indianapolis, Indiana; and Grundy Center, Iowa—had provided a lot of evidence of the success of the New PE. Lawler was convinced that he and PE4life were now armed with enough evidence from their breakthrough PE programs that they could persuade school administrators, board members, and parents around the country to find ways to make fitness-based PE part of their school's curriculums.

However, as Lawler took his message to school administrators around the country, his message met resistance. The administrators he talked to were indeed impressed with the results he was presenting related to health and wellness; however, they were also feeling pressure from school board members and parents to get their school's academic assessment scores up. Lawler was told that this pressure for improved academic performance would prevent adding time for physical education. In fact, he discovered that despite the health and wellness data he was presenting, some administrators and school board members were actually cutting the time allotted for physical education.

It became apparent to Lawler that the state assessment tests inspired by No Child Left Behind were the true scoreboard that was driving the decision making of principals. Administrators thought they needed to find more class time for math, science, and language arts to boost standardized test scores. As a result, they often cut or dropped PE to find that time. Lawler now fully realized that it was going to take more than developing healthier kids to start a full-fledged physical education revolution.

Lawler was frustrated. If the powerful health-related results he was getting in his PE4life program—in the face of an increasing number of stories in the media about the declining health of our children and a childhood obesity epidemic—weren't enough to start a New PE revolution, then what was?

He'd find his answer one evening while sitting in his den and listening to the radio.

4

FIT KIDS PERFORM BETTER ACADEMICALLY

> "**B**ecause of the increased reliance on test scores for school survival, many [school] districts across the nation are getting rid of physical education and recess. Given the powerful cognitive effects of physical activity, this makes no sense. Cutting off physical exercise—the very activity most likely to promote cognitive performance—to do better on a test score is like trying to gain weight by starving yourself."
>
> —*Dr. John Medina, neuroscientist and author of* Brain Rules

Phil Lawler walked into his den, flipped on the radio, and sat down at his desk to do some paperwork. He was vaguely aware that his radio was tuned to National Public Radio. He picked up on the fact that the host and his guest were talking about the workings of the brain. Occasionally, he'd hear something of interest, but for the most part, the radio was little more than background noise.

Then he heard the show's guest say something that stopped him in his tracks and sent a jolt of excitement through his body.

"Exercise is like Miracle-Gro for the brain," said the guest. "It grows brain cells."

Lawler was now deeply interested in the radio program. He stopped what he was doing and began listening to the show intently. It turns out that the show's guest was Dr. John Ratey, a professor of psychiatry at Harvard Medical School and an expert on exercise's impact on the brain.

"When I heard Ratey talk about exercise being Miracle-Gro for the brain on the radio, I thought it was one of the most exciting things I'd ever heard," recalled Lawler. "I quickly started using the 'Miracle-Gro' line in all my talks and discussions about quality, fitness-based PE. I could now talk about exercise's benefits for the brain as well as the body.

"It was perfect timing because I'd grown a little frustrated that schools were slow to adopt our PE4life philosophy. I thought once we came out with the data that our program had a rate of 3 percent overweight and obese students compared to a national average of 35 percent that schools and communities around the country would be lined up to see what we were doing and how they could adopt our program.

"Unfortunately, that wasn't the case. However, I felt Ratey's comment about the positive benefits of exercise on the brain could be the breakthrough we needed."

Not long after Lawler heard Ratey on the NPR program, Ratey serendipitously discovered Lawler by virtue of the movie *Supersize Me,* a documentary in which the director and star, Morgan Spurlock, eats exclusively from the McDonald's menu for 30 days and watches his health decline in the process. Lawler had a bit role in the documentary and a longer appearance in a bonus segment on the DVD version of the film.

"My daughter's friend saw *Supersize Me* and told my daughter about it," recalls Ratey. "My daughter thought I'd be interested. I got the DVD and found the movie interesting. But I was most intrigued by the passionate physical education teacher I saw on the DVD. He was passionate about the importance of fitness for all students. I had my assistant call Phil Lawler to find out a little more about his program.

"Well, she was blown away by Phil. She called me back and said, 'You have an appointment to talk to him tomorrow, and I have you booked on a plane to go visit his school. I think this is just what you need to illustrate the effects of exercise on learning.'"

Lawler called Ratey the following day at the scheduled time. He gave Ratey his typical two-hour passionate spiel about his physical education program in Naperville, Illinois. He talked about all the amazing benefits that he was seeing with students and in the community because of the school's daily fitness-based physical education program.

"When my assistant booked a trip for me to go see the program in Naperville before I'd even talked to Phil, I pushed back a little," says Ratey. "After I spoke with Phil, I was ready to go right after the call."

A week later, Ratey flew into Chicago and made the short drive to Naperville, a nice bedroom community north of Chicago.

"I fell in love with what I saw at Madison Junior High School and Naperville Central High School," said Ratey. "I wish we'd had a video camera to tape the shock and amazement on my face during my first meeting with

Phil and Paul (Zientarski), including the tour of the PE programs at those schools."

Lawler was equally excited about meeting Ratey.

"Getting Ratey interested and involved in our program was huge," said Lawler. "Our PE4life philosophy wasn't expanding around the country as fast as I hoped. Despite our great results, I thought people were being too slow to adopt the principles in their schools and communities. At that time, we were focusing solely on the health and wellness benefits of PE4life, and we would always get a push back from principals because of the pressure on them to raise academic test scores. They just didn't see how they could justify carving out more time for PE despite the fitness and health benefits. Well, Ratey and his research gave us a chance to expand the conversation to include the benefits of exercise on the brain and academic performance."

After Ratey returned to Massachusetts, Lawler began to hound him about the latest research on exercise's benefits for the brain and learning. Ratey and his assistant kept feeding Lawler new ammunition to support his case that fitness-based PE enhances academic performance. Ratey, in turn, wanted to learn more about Lawler and his Naperville PE4life Academy Training Center.

Ratey became so intrigued with Lawler's work that a case study on Naperville School District 203's physical education program became the first chapter in Ratey's book *SPARK: The Revolutionary New Science of Exercise and the Brain*.

"I had put *SPARK* on the back burner until I talked to Phil," says Ratey. "The book was smoldering, but it wasn't front and center in my life until Phil came along."

Zientarski, who was once slow to come around to Lawler's urgings to change his PE model to one based on health and wellness rather than sports, was now a New PE zealot to rival Lawler. He was completely on board with the importance of the new brain research and what it could mean for quality physical education programs.

Together, these two fitness-based PE disciples began reading neuroscience research papers, attending research seminars on the brain, and regularly calling experts such as Ratey and others—not typical endeavors for K-12 physical education teachers.

What they discovered about exercise's positive impact on the brain would change their careers as physical educators. It would transform their subject—physical education—from the "Rodney Dangerfield of education," as Lawler would often call it, into a subject with the potential to transform how K-12 education is delivered in this country.

The building block of learning is the wiring together of brain cells or neurons. Physical exercise facilitates this wiring by stimulating the production and release of a number of key chemicals such as BDNF, a protein that encourages brain cells to wire together and multiply.

As such, cardiovascular activity results in increased brain functioning during cognitively challenging tasks. Bottom line, students are more ready to learn after exercise. Exercise, it turns out, is the perfect learning readiness tool.

One study, led by neuroscientist Arthur Kramer of the University of Illinois, found that as little as three hours a week of aerobic exercise increased the brain's volume of gray matter (neurons) and white matter (connections between neurons).

"After only three months, the people who exercised had the brain volumes of people three years younger," said Kramer.

Lawler and Zientarski found the evidence from school settings to be just as compelling. For example, a 2002 California Department of Education study found a direct correlation between higher levels of physical fitness and higher academic test scores among 5th and 9th graders. The study was replicated in 2004 with strikingly similar results. As fitness levels rose, so did test scores.

Delaine Eastin, California state superintendent of public instruction at the time of the studies, said, "We now have the proof we've been looking for: Students achieve best when they are physically fit."

In Titusville, Pennsylvania, standardized test scores have jumped from below the state average to 17 and 18 percent above average in reading and math, respectively, since the implementation of a PE4life program.

The remarkable findings aren't just coming from the United States. In a Copenhagen study, students who participated in an intense physical activity program five days a week saw their grades improve an average of 1.5 letter grades.

"I get about 40 to 50 research papers a week on some aspect of how exercise affects the brain," says Ratey. "Less than a decade ago, I would only see a couple a month. In the field of neuroscience, exercise and the brain is one of the hottest areas going."

During the six months following their meeting with Ratey, Lawler and Zientarski began calling or e-mailing each other with their latest findings on exercise's positive impact on the brain. They constantly kept each other energized about the possibilities. They began brainstorming about ways they could incorporate the brain research discoveries into their programs. Lawler also worked with PE4life on incorporating the findings on exercise and the brain into PE4life's presentations and meetings with teachers, administrators, school board members, parents, and the media.

Today, the research on exercise as powerful medicine for the brain has gone mainstream. For example, Stanford Medical School held a symposium in August 2009 entitled "Exercise and the Brain." It was a breakthrough event—the first time an entire major medical conference was held with a focus on exercise's impact on the brain.

Lawler had a difficult time containing his enthusiasm about the many ways that exercise can get students ready to learn.

"What the research is showing is that exercise optimizes learning in multiple ways," said Lawler. "Besides creating new brain cells, exercise improves behavior, impulse control, attention, motivation, and boosts self-esteem. It regulates anxiety and combats depression and the toxic effects of stress. It increases arousal and lessens fatigue. If a pharmaceutical company came up with a drug that had those benefits, it would be the blockbuster drug of all time!"

> **B**esides creating new brain cells, exercise improves behavior, impulse control, attention, motivation, and boosts self-esteem.

Lawler's ongoing relationship with Dr. Kenneth Cooper played a big role in the development of a landmark study on the relationship between fitness levels and academic performance in Texas schools. The 2008 Cooper Youth Fitness Study in Texas added to the foundation established by the California studies that showed a very strong link between fitness and academic performance.

Like California, the Texas study found that the better a student's fitness score on the Fitnessgram test was, the better he or she performed in math and language. Other findings related to learning were also noteworthy: The higher the fitness levels, the fewer the discipline incidents (e.g., drugs, alcohol, violence, truancy, and so on), and the better the school attendance.

Perhaps the most exciting finding from Cooper's Texas study was that the strong correlation between fitness and academic performance held true regardless of ethnicity, race, or size of the school.

When Texas schools were stratified by the state rating system (exemplary, recognized, acceptable, and unacceptable), the schools with the highest and lowest levels of academic performance were the schools that also had the highest and lowest levels of cardiovascular fitness, respectively.

Cooper is always quick to point out that his work in Texas was spurred by Lawler's efforts in Naperville.

"The programs in Naperville were the basis for our work here in Texas with physical education," says Cooper. "I used Lawler's work and great experience in the field to set up the programs we have in Texas."

Making the Texas study a reality required that Cooper undertake a huge battle with the Texas legislature. Cooper fought to get Fitnessgram testing in each of the 9,000 schools in Texas. He faced a stiff fight from a variety of angles, including a group of Texas school administrators who said that No Child Left Behind demanded that they focus on math, science, and English.

"They said, 'We'll eliminate it,'" recalls Cooper. "'We have no room for it in the curriculum.' They fought me like crazy. But I had the Texas Medical Association, Diabetes Association, and Heart Association behind me. They all saw the tremendous need for it."

Cooper finally gained enough support in the Texas legislature to pass his bill, but he was told that the state simply couldn't fund it during an economic crisis.

"I stood before the legislature on four different occasions testifying," says Cooper. "Finally, it came to this ultimatum: 'There's no funding from the state, you've got to do it yourself.' I said, 'Okay, if that's the requirement, I will raise the money myself.' I went on the warpath and raised 3.1 million dollars."

Thanks to Cooper and his persistence, the state of Texas now has important evidence that physical fitness is not only important for student wellness but for optimal learning as well.

One study on exercise and the brain that had a particularly strong impact on both Lawler and Zientarski was conducted not too far from Naperville at the University of Illinois. As part of this study, 21 students were asked to memorize a string of letters and then pick them out from a list flashed at them. At that point, they were required to do one of three things for 30 minutes—sit quietly, run on a treadmill, or lift weights—before performing the letter test again. After a 30-minute cool-down, they were tested once again.

On the following two days, the students returned to do the post-memorization options—sitting quietly, running, or lifting weights—that they hadn't done previously. The students were noticeably quicker and more accurate on the retest after running on the treadmill versus lifting weights or sitting quietly. And the runners continued to perform better when tested after the 30-minute cool-down period.

This test mirrored similar studies by concluding that it was aerobic exercise, not weightlifting or any other type of exercise, that had the most positive impact on the brain. For one, although all types of exercise appear to have multiple benefits, it's aerobic exercise that grows brain cells and makes the brain more ready to learn in a variety of ways.

"There seems to be something different about aerobic exercise," says Charles Hillman, an associate professor in the department of kinesiology at the University of Illinois and an author of the study.

Other scientists at the University of Illinois found similar results in a study with an elderly population. Aerobic activity improved cognitive abilities, while an exercise program based on stretching did not.

A review of research on exercise and the brain published in the summer of 2009 by the Association for Psychological Science found that studies in both animals and humans "overwhelmingly" indicate that exercise helps

Phil always emphasized that aerobic exercise encourages the growth of brain cells. Offering a variety of cardio equipment in your PE program will keep kids' bodies as well as brains active.

the brain. Kramer, one of the article's authors, says that there's now enough evidence to launch a public policy campaign that includes an endorsement of aerobic exercise to improve brain function.

In a landmark report released in April 2010, the Centers for Disease Control and Prevention (CDC) concluded, "There is substantial evidence that physical activity can help improve academic achievement (including grades and standardized test scores)."

After digging through the research on exercise and the brain, Zientarski and Lawler came up with a way to incorporate their learning into the educational process at Naperville Central High School. They launched a pilot test at Central called Zero-Hour PE.

Central took a group of ninth grade students who were reading below grade level and divided them into two groups. The first group took a literacy class only, and the second group took a PE class focused on cardiovascular fitness immediately before their literacy class. The PE class was held before the first official school period of the day, hence the name Zero-Hour PE.

During their exercise sessions, Zero-Hour PE students were required to use heart rate monitors and keep their heart rates between 80 and 90 percent of their maximum heart rate.

At the end of the semester, the Zero-Hour PE group showed a 17 percent improvement in reading and comprehension, compared to their peers who took the literacy class only and showed a 10.7 percent improvement. In one semester, those with Zero-Hour PE (now called *Learning Readiness PE*) increased their reading and comprehension scores by 1.4 on a grade-level equivalency scale.

In a similar follow-up study done at Central, students enrolled in a PE class immediately before a math class increased their score on an algebra readiness assessment by an average of 20 percent—compared to 4 percent for the students who took PE several hours *after* the same math class.

Another experiment at Central involved splitting literacy students into two groups: one group taking Zero-Hour PE and then taking the literacy class immediately afterward and one group taking Zero-Hour PE but not taking their literacy class until the last period of the day. As expected, the group who took the literacy class immediately after Zero-Hour PE did significantly better.

"Multiple studies have now shown that the more physically active and fit kids are, the better they perform academically," says Zientarski. "It's part of why our students do as well as they do—it's a total mind, total body educational approach.

"The tipping point for this revolution was the brain research connecting exercise with academic performance."

The findings were enough for Central's administration to formally create a Learning Readiness PE class. Furthermore, the success of the Learning Readiness PE program has benefited all students at Naperville Central.

"Guidance counselors at Naperville Central now suggest that all students schedule their toughest subjects immediately after physical education, to capitalize on the beneficial effects of exercise," said Lawler.

Learning readiness appears to be the perfect description for what fitness-based PE accomplishes.

"In our department, we create brain cells," says Zientarski smiling. "It's up to the other teachers to fill them."

Zientarski traces Naperville's successful Learning Readiness PE program back to Lawler's initiative in contacting Dr. Ratey.

"Phil got Ratey here," says Zientarski. "If Ratey never comes here, Zero-Hour PE never happens."

Given the growing number of findings on the positive impact of aerobic exercise on learning, it's shocking to note that in parts of the United States, elementary schools are being built without gyms. The trend of having less—

not more—physical education and recess is exactly the opposite of what the research is suggesting in order to optimize students' readiness to learn.

Consider recess. According to Stuart Brown, MD, author of the book *Play,* the more recess time students get, the better behaved and attentive they are. He pointed to a study reporting that a minimum of 30 minutes of recess is necessary in order to optimize learning factors such as class behavior and paying attention.

According to Ratey, there is one school tradition that needs to go the way of the dinosaur, and it's not recess. It's "time-outs."

"Time-outs and no recess penalties are the worst things you can do for misbehaving, inattentive kids," says Ratey. "They need to go to a 'Time-In' situation instead."

"Time-In" is an innovative solution for inattentive kids developed at Tavelli Elementary School in Fort Collins, Colorado. At Tavelli, overactive, inattentive, or disruptive students are sent to a small room to exercise for 5 to 10 minutes on a mini-trampoline, a Dance Dance Revolution game, or a similar device before returning to the classroom.

According to Dr. Ratey, this type of short exercise break switches on a part of the brain that's been "sleeping." When the switch goes on, the student is less fidgety and more attentive.

"The power of 'Time-In' isn't that it burns off excess energy," says Ratey. "It's that the short exercise break turns on the attention system in the brain and also works to inhibit impulse actions."

Dan Lawler, PhD, is the recently retired long-time principal of Tavelli Elementary in Fort Collins, Colorado. He also happens to be Phil Lawler's brother. As a result, he heard Phil's passionate arguments for aerobic exercise in the school setting for many years—on the phone, at holiday dinners, at baseball games, and so on.

It took awhile, but Phil convinced Dan in 2002. At that time, Dan decided to make Tavelli a wellness-based elementary school. He created a wellness committee made up of teachers, parents, and community members. He instituted 10 minutes of aerobic exercise to start the school day in every classroom, every morning. He had the same 10-minute "Spark" break in the afternoon. Spark time involved playing an aerobics video on classroom television monitors in each room as a way to prepare the brain for learning.

He also brought in wellness experts to speak to students about making smart lifestyle choices to prevent obesity, diabetes, heart disease, and other health problems.

Perhaps most impressively, he created an exercise learning lab filled with approximately 20 pieces of equipment that engage the students in brain-stimulating games while they exercise aerobically. The exercise learning lab is the first of its kind in a school setting. Students are scheduled to participate in the lab several times a week—in addition to their regular PE time. A sign in the lab reads, "Mens sana in corpore sano . . . A sound mind in a sound body."

"The lab has been very popular. Kids have fun and gain fitness, health, academic, and behavior benefits," says Dan Lawler.

Over an eight-year period, a wellness lifestyle has been embedded in the Tavelli culture, improving the lives of students in multiple ways. It's also become an unintended marketing tool.

"An interesting side effect of our transitioning to a wellness school is that we now have parents seeking our school out for their children," says Dan Lawler. "They want to be part of a school that addresses the whole student. Our 'wellness brand' became very powerful."

Movement is the key. A high-quality, daily, fitness-based physical education program is the ideal, but even seemingly small interventions that make the body move a little have a positive effect. For example, one study found that having kids sit on balls instead of in chairs helps academic performance. Another study found that kids who used standing desks instead of sitting desks performed 7 to 10 percent better.

Sadly, in too many schools today, there's a tremendous shortage of physical activity among our young people.

"Given what we know about exercise's positive impact on the brain and learning, combined with declines in physical education and recess time, we could file a class-action malpractice lawsuit against American educators due to the lack of physical activity in schools," said Phil Lawler.

Neuroscience is the biggest ally in supporting the link between movement and learning, according to Jean Blaydes-Madigan, a pioneer in teaching academic subjects kinesthetically and a long-time colleague of Lawler's. Madigan created an action-based learning program for teachers that uses movement to prepare the brain for learning. It also anchors learning through the physical.

"It's clear that movement facilitates cognition," says Blaydes-Madigan. "It improves memory and retention while reinforcing the classroom teacher's math, language arts, science, and social studies objectives. The question I try to get classroom teachers to ask of themselves and their students as a first step is 'How can we do this lesson standing up?'"

Ratey wholeheartedly agrees.

"Movement enhances learning. For example, I think the evidence is clear that 45 minutes a day of physical education doesn't take away from a student's academic prowess—as some school principals and parents fear; it improves it," says Ratey.

As the CDC report points out, the link between physical activity, including physical education, and academic performance is strong.

"There's so much research out there that says healthy, active children learn better," says VanLengen. "If we spend all our school time having students at their desks sitting and studying, they're not going to be as effective as if they actually were exercising and preparing their minds to learn. It's one of the biggest challenges PE4life faces as an organization—convincing administrators to make more time in their schedules for physical education. Administrators want to devote as much time as possible to classroom learning, which, again, is understandable based on the pressures they face, but it's misguided.

"I think the real opportunity to change the culture in schools is to illuminate the evidence showing that healthy, active kids learn better, and that exercise prepares the brain for work in a classroom."

Ratey says it doesn't take a lot of physical activity to make a difference.

"When standing and doing minimal movement around a standing desk, your brain works 7 percent to 10 percent better," says Ratey. "If you want to help dyslexic children read, have them standing and reading."

According to Dr. John Medina, a developmental molecular biologist and author of the best-selling book *Brain Rules,* "If you wanted to create an education environment that was directly opposed to what the brain was good at doing, you probably would design something like a classroom."

In *Brain Rules,* Medina discusses the ramifications for the world of education resulting from the growing mound of research on exercise's impact on the brain.

"It might even reintroduce the notion of school uniforms," says Medina. "Of what would the new apparel consist? Simply gym clothes, worn all day long."

The evidence strongly suggests that the research on exercise and the brain is going to change the education profession.

And Ratey believes that Lawler was leading the way.

"It's amazing that Phil Lawler, a gym teacher, is revolutionizing education—not just physical education but all of education," said Ratey.

5

A MAGIC BULLET FOR BEHAVIORAL ISSUES

> **"I** tell people that going for a run is like taking a little bit of Prozac and a little bit of Ritalin because, like the drugs, exercise elevates neurotransmitters. It's a handy metaphor to get the point across, but the deeper explanation is that exercise balances neurotransmitters—along with the rest of the neurochemicals in the brain. And as you'll see, keeping your brain in balance can change your life."
>
> —*Dr. John Ratey, clinical associate professor of psychiatry at Harvard Medical School*

The more Lawler dug into the brain research, the more he was convinced that between the benefits for health and wellness and the benefits for academic performance, he had all the ammunition he needed to convince principals and school board members to make quality daily PE a reality. Then he discovered the third leg of the exercise triad: the positive benefits of exercise on student behavior. Now he was convinced that exercise would eventually revolutionize education.

PE4life had recently partnered with Kansas City area funders to create a PE4life Academy Training Center in an urban core school in the Kansas City, Missouri, school district. Lawler was excited about the prospect because for years he'd believed that a fitness-based physical education program would have significant effects on students no matter what a school's socioeconomic situation might be. PE4life Academy Training Centers were thriving in Titusville, Pennsylvania (an old oil town that had fallen on hard times) and Grundy Center, Iowa (a farming town so small that it's not even on some maps of Iowa), in addition to the flagship academy in Naperville, Illinois.

The statistics on wellness *and* academic performance had improved in Titusville and Grundy Center, just as they had in Naperville. Lawler expected the same thing to happen in Kansas City.

"Whenever I spoke with news reporters or attendees at our trainings in Naperville, inevitably someone would ask 'Do you think a program like this could work in a poor inner-city situation?'" said Lawler. "I always said 'Yes,' but I didn't have any hard evidence."

Lawler was hopeful that Woodland Elementary in Kansas City would provide that evidence.

PE4life's Brenda VanLengen had been working with Kansas City community and school leaders for over a year looking for a potential site for a PE4life Academy Training Center. When she found some generous local foundation support from the Kansas City philanthropic community, she turned to Woodland because she knew she had two critical pieces in place: a PE staff that believed in PE4life's fitness-based physical education philosophy and a committed principal.

"Woodland's PE staff was going to do whatever it took to get a PE4life Academy Training Center," said Lawler. "They had a basement, which was basically a boiler room that had become a storage area for old desks and shelves and things like that. They cleaned that out and spruced it up a bit and converted it into a fitness center for the PE department."

PE4life also had outstanding support from Woodland principal Craig Rupert, who was creative in finding more time for physical education in the school day.

"For a PE4life program to be successful, the principal has to be completely on board," says Brenda VanLengen, former chief design officer and now vice-chair of the board for PE4life. "The administrative support at Woodland has been terrific."

Before the school integrated the PE4life Core Principles, Woodland students had participated in one 50-minute physical education class per week. As part of the new fitness-based physical education program, Woodland hired one additional physical education instructor. In addition, Rupert found time to offer physical education every day for 45 minutes. The school also upgraded facilities, brought in new interactive fitness equipment and assessment technology (such as heart rate monitors and pedometers), and incorporated PE4life's fitness-based philosophy into the delivery of PE.

For the first year, all fourth and fifth graders at Woodland were tested with the Fitnessgram assessment to measure fitness levels across six health and fitness indicators before starting the new PE program. They were measured on the same assessment after one year. All six indicators saw significant improvement. Of particular note, cardiovascular fitness improved 207 percent.

Those results could be somewhat expected when increasing physical activity exponentially. However, one group of results was attention grabbing: the indicators for disciplinary issues. Rupert included the discipline indicators because he wanted to see if integrating the PE4life Core Principles would have any impact on student behavior. It did. Discipline incidents involving violence dropped 59 percent, and out-of-school suspension days went down 67 percent. After two years of the program, the average annual number of discipline incidents is down 51 percent from pre-PE4life days, and the average annual out-of-school suspensions number is down 60 percent.

"It's not just the increased levels of fitness we are seeing in our kids which has everyone excited," says Rupert. "Students are also more motivated throughout the day, their enthusiasm is way up, and discipline issues are way down."

When Lawler saw the impact of the PE4life Core Principles on student behavior at Woodland, he felt the same surge of excitement that he had the first time he heard Dr. Ratey talking about exercise as "Miracle-Gro for the brain."

"I was thrilled," said Lawler. "It was a terrific finding. The data on behavioral issues kind of happened by accident. PE4life was focusing on training the trainers who would then impact the fitness scores. It was the Woodland administration that decided to keep track of behavioral issues before and after the PE4life Core Principles were integrated."

Lawler had heard a few anecdotes about PE4life Core Principles reducing disciplinary problems, but he'd never seen any hard data to support the hypothesis.

For example, Tim McCord, the PE4life Academy director in Titusville, Pennsylvania, once told Lawler that the middle school's principal said that after implementing the PE4life program, the school went an entire year without a fight in the school. The principal told McCord that in addition to the benefits to the brain from higher fitness levels, she believed that integrating the PE4life principles leveled the playing field for her middle school students and helped lead to an elimination of cliques. She thought that was a major reason for the reduction in fights.

But that was an anecdotal account based on speculation and an isolated observation. The Woodland study was much more substantive.

"Right away, I thought *We got something here,*" said Lawler. "If we could show that quality physical education could result in improved wellness, increased academic performance, *and* a drop in disciplinary issues, we would have something that any school board member, principal, teacher, or parent should be interested in. Once we found out about it, we made it a big part of our message. We now had the perfect exercise triad: improved learning, behavior, and wellness."

Brain researchers such as Ratey and Medina aren't surprised at all by findings like those from Woodland Elementary.

"Kids are less likely to be disruptive in terms of their classroom behaviors when they have been active," according to Medina.

A couple real-world examples illustrate this perfectly.

Allison Cameron is a teacher at City Park Collegiate High School, a Canadian alternative high school for kids of last resort in Saskatoon, Saskatchewan. She teaches grade 8 students, almost all of whom have learning disabilities, behavioral problems, or domestic or personal issues. Many have defiance disorders. In addition, approximately 50 percent have ADHD. Her students often have anger issues that prevent them from learning properly. Class disruptions are commonplace at this school. Most of her students are doing work at the grade 4 level.

Cameron has a background in sports and fitness. Through her readings, she learned that special ed students have fewer behavioral problems after going out for a jog. Grant Roberts, a friend of Cameron's and a personal fitness trainer and health club owner, told her about the Naperville district 203 program run by Lawler and Zientarski. She contacted Zientarski and later Lawler. After each conversation, she came away excited about the possibilities for her school. Zientarski and Lawler invited her to their annual DuPage County physical education conference. It was there that she learned about Dr. John Ratey and his book *SPARK*.

After attending the DuPage conference and reading *SPARK,* Cameron was convinced she needed to implement a movement-based initiative at City Park Collegiate High School. When Roberts' fitness organization donated eight treadmills and six exercise bikes, Cameron was off and running— literally. She got administrative approval to place the exercise equipment in the back of her classroom, and the bikes and treadmills became part of her teaching approach.

As with any new activity that Cameron introduced, the students were skeptical, and some were outright defiant, refusing to get on a bike or treadmill. Gradually, the students got on board. They saw Cameron doing the workouts every day and began to see the benefits in the handful of students who had been doing the workouts from the first day. Slowly but surely, all the students began to participate in the exercise segments.

Some started by doing only 5 minutes of slow walking. Eventually, Cameron was able to get her class to consistently keep their heart rates in the 65 to 75 percent of maximum range for 20 minutes. She found that sustained aerobic movement for 20 minutes was the key to the program's success. She's discovered that 20 minutes of aerobic exercise results in 2 hours of sustained concentration from her students. Thus, she believes that the high state of learning readiness that follows the exercise more than compensates for the 20 minutes of instruction time that is lost to exercise.

During a typical day, the first thing Cameron's students do is 20 minutes of cardio exercise with heart rate monitors on. They are then prepared for academic work. Since Cameron began her "exercise for learning" program, her students are focusing better and working harder, and they are less defiant. The swearing and running around in class that used to be commonplace have dropped dramatically.

"It feels great," says Alex Herbel (age 14), one of Cameron's students who was bullied at his former school and suffered from concentration problems. "I feel better about myself. I didn't think anything like this would help, but it does. It's crazy."

After only four months, Cameron's students improved a full grade level on average in reading, writing, and math. That's a huge leap forward for kids who began Cameron's exercise program three or four grade levels behind their peers. The only change Cameron made was adding the aerobic exercise component to her classroom.

"We had a lot of added benefits besides improved academic performance," says Cameron. "Especially in the areas of behavior and attention."

Dr. Ratey was not surprised by Cameron's results at City Park Collegiate.

"After exercise, students are sharper, more attentive, less impulsive and fidgety, and sustain their attention longer," says Ratey. "What I find so compelling is the strong relationship between movement and attention."

> **After exercise, students are sharper, more attentive, less impulsive and fidgety, and sustain their attention longer.**

Cameron saw enormous potential in her students but wasn't sure how to bring it out.

"It's so difficult to effectively teach in a school considered the last resort," says Cameron.

Then she started her exercise program. After initiating her "treadmill classroom," her students gradually began to transform before her eyes.

"How do you put into words the profound experience of witnessing the metamorphosis of a human being whose potential emerges before your eyes?" asks Cameron. "If I hadn't seen it with my own eyes, I wouldn't have believed it.

"Everyone changed. Kids started getting off Ritalin. They started coming to school every day to use the workout equipment. A student who could barely sit still for 10 to 15 minutes could sit quietly and complete an assignment for the first time. Students could concentrate and work harder. There was no swearing, no running around. One student felt more energized and with improved mood could control his anger and concentrate better. One student said he started getting smarter, paid attention more, and began to see how he could turn his life around. Not to mention an improvement in reading and writing of 25 to 30 percent. One student had a 400 percent increase in comprehension. Math performance was up 25 percent."

Cameron says that the benefits of exercise are well known but that the traditional competitive sport approach is designed to fail with a lot of kids.

"Kids who aren't athletically inclined tend to shy away from it," says Cameron. "On a track, the slower people get lapped, and it can be damaging to their self-esteem. In this (program), no one knows who's slower or faster."

◆ ◆ ◆ ◆ ◆ ◆ ◆ ◆ ◆ ◆ ◆ ◆

After 33 years spent as a teacher, counselor, and coach, David Spurlock was named coordinator of physical education for the Charleston County School District in Charleston, South Carolina. His goal was to make physical education more relevant in the district.

"I knew I couldn't make PE important to administrators unless I found something besides the old way we'd always taught PE," says Spurlock. "I even needed to find something to lean on besides the fitness and health of the child."

He didn't know what that something was, but he started looking for cutting-edge approaches to physical education. While doing his research, he came across Phil Lawler, Paul Zientarski, and the Naperville 203 School District physical education program. After initial conversations with Zientarski and Lawler, Spurlock attended Zientarski and Lawler's DuPage County Physical Education Institute.

"I was truly inspired," says Spurlock. "What I learned was that Phil and Paul were changing the face of physical education and how it's looked at. I learned that if physical education was done right, it could lead to very good academic and behavioral outcomes."

Spurlock followed up his visit to Naperville with multiple phone conversations with Lawler and Zientarski.

"I spent hours with David talking about ways he could apply the learnings from Naperville to his unique situation in Charleston," said Lawler.

Spurlock decided to do a pilot test with one of his most challenging situations: Charleston Progressive Academy (CPA). CPA is a Title 1 school with 80 percent of the students on free or reduced lunches. The school serves students in fourth through eighth grades.

Before Spurlock's New PE intervention, whenever CPA teachers encountered discipline problems, they would write up referrals on the students involved and send the referrals to the principal. Students who received a written referral had to go to school before class started in the morning and sit in the cafeteria, where they would be told to read, be quiet, and not move.

Spurlock and the CPA physical education teacher created a new intake program they called AM EX (morning exercise) to replace the old morning referral program. Instead of going to the cafeteria to sit, the intake kids were taken to the gym and given various aerobic activities to participate in for 40 minutes. Activities included basketball, DDR, pogo stick jumping, and jump roping.

First-year results were astounding. Disciplinary referrals had dropped 49 percent. School suspensions were down 60 percent. The AM EX program was the only intervention implemented.

Once again, Spurlock's findings were consistent with the findings of researchers Medina and Ratey.

"Kids feel better about themselves (after exercise); they have better self-esteem, have less depression, and less anxiety," says Medina.

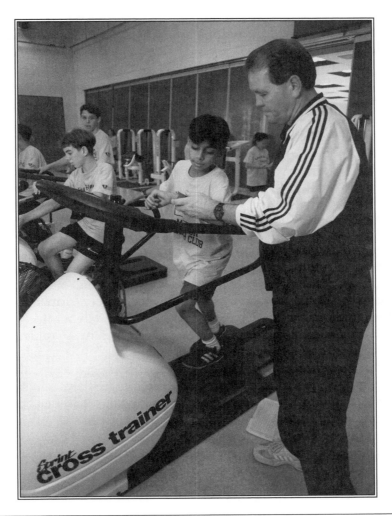

Heart rate monitors tell how hard a student is working. Fit kids feel better about themselves mentally, emotionally, and physically, so it is important to help them understand how to work within their target heart rate zone.

"Twelve minutes of exercise at 85 percent of your maximum heart rate is like taking a little bit of Prozac and a little bit of Ritalin in a very holistic manner," adds Ratey.

"We were thrilled with the impact of the AM EX program," says Spurlock. "We quickly began exploring ways to take the Naperville PE4life concepts to other schools in the district."

◇ ◇ ◇ ◇ ◇ ◇ ◇ ◇ ◇ ◇ ◇

Dan Connor is the principal at R.B. Stall High School, which is one of Spurlock's schools in Charleston County. Connor was intrigued by the results at CPA, enough so that he and a group of colleagues visited Naperville to see the PE4life programs and to talk with Lawler and Zientarski.

"We're a Palmetto Priority School, which essentially communicates we have high poverty and low test scores," says Connor.

After being inspired by the Naperville PE4life Academy Training Center, Connor and Stall High School were fortunate to become the beneficiaries of a $10,000 gift from the Medical Society of South Carolina. They used this gift to start a fitness room and a PE4life-based program. Connor has seen benefits throughout his school as a result of the new fitness room and the PE4life philosophy. But he's most excited about what the fitness-based PE program has done for his special-needs students.

"The biggest bang has come from our special-needs kids," says Connor. "Nothing short of amazing and closer to miraculous. Last year we instituted a mandatory time every day that our autistic and TMD kids could use the fitness room. I literally watched several youngsters who barely communicated begin to smile and interact with people. It was amazing! Some of our parents were stunned by the transformation that took place with their kids. It was more than the proverbial light switch going on for a couple kids. It was as if they had a complete personality makeover. How cool is that?"

Spurlock and the Charleston County School District continue to expand their PE-based programs, including Learning Readiness PE and Action-Based Learning programs.

"What Lawler and his team started in Naperville is amazing," said Spurlock. "Naperville is the Mecca of PE for me. Phil Lawler has been the impetus for what we've done here. He's the reason I'm trying to do this here. Based on all I've learned from Phil and the Naperville team, I've started calling myself a neurokinesiologist now instead of a PE teacher!"

Lawler was proud of the work he did with fitness-based physical education and movement-based learning initiatives. He was passionate about speaking to educators and parents about how exercise improves learning readiness, makes kids healthier, improves behavior, and boosts mood. But he was also thrilled with what all the research and outcomes have meant to the self-esteem of physical education teachers.

"For decades, physical education teachers were the 'Rodney Danger-fields of education,' no respect," said Lawler. "Now because of the growing mound of research touting the benefits of exercise and movement in the educational setting, I think physical education is the most important course in the school. And I get a great deal of joy when I see PE teachers realizing that."

Lawler believed that advocates of fitness-based PE and more physical activity in the classroom have the perfect case to sell: Exercise improves learning, behavior, and wellness.

"What more can we ask for?" asked Lawler. "If we can't convince administrators and parents of the benefits of fitness-based PE and movement-based learning initiatives, then we need better sales skills, not more evidence. Our product is fine, and we have all the research we need to support it."

chapter

6

A PASSIONATE CONNECTOR

> **"P**hil Lawler was a networker. This was truly Phil's gift.
> He reached out to people from all over the country
> and the world. Once he got in touch with you, he never
> lost touch. Everyone became wound up in his web.
> He kept connecting the dots and putting people
> in touch with others in his network."
>
> —*Paul Zientarski, physical education department chair,*
> *Naperville Central High School*

If you ask people who knew him to identify the first two things that come to mind when they hear the name Phil Lawler, they will usually say "passion" first and "connector" second.

If "Phil Lawler" was an entry in the dictionary, those two words—*passion* and *connector*—would come close to perfectly describing the man.

And if you could only pick one word, it would have to be *passion*.

"Phil Lawler has this passion to improve the lives of kids," said Brenda VanLengen. "When I think of Phil, the first thing that comes to mind would be his passion—his passion for life and his passion for helping kids be more active and healthy."

Phil Lawler's passion for his cause inspired even the most passionate and successful people, including people such as Dr. Kenneth Cooper and Dr. John Ratey. In fact, what Lawler accomplished in the physical education field in general—and with his Naperville 203 PE program specifically—inspired Cooper to raise approximately $3 million to test the fitness levels of 2.6 million Texas schoolchildren.

"Phil Lawler's ideas have been creative," said Cooper, who's often referred to as the "Father of Aerobics." "They've been successful.

"I've visited Phil Lawler in Naperville several times. I saw his excitement. He took me around the gymnasium there and showed me all they do. They're way ahead of everybody else. I could see the passion he had about what they're doing. What was equally as exciting to me is seeing the response of the students. They loved that guy."

Ratey was so inspired by Lawler and his PE program that after returning from his visit to Naperville, he made completing his book, *SPARK: The Revolutionary New Science of Exercise and the Brain,* a priority. *SPARK* was a book he'd started years before but had placed on the back burner until meeting Lawler and seeing his program.

In fact, Ratey made the Naperville story the first chapter in *SPARK,* and Lawler was one of three people he dedicated the book to (Cooper and neuroscientist Carl Cotman were the other two).

"I have the ultimate reverence for Phil Lawler," said Ratey. "He's a revolutionary and an incredible salesman because he has so much passion."

"He's relentless," added Todd Whitthorne, president and CEO of Cooper Concepts, Inc. "I wouldn't say he's maniacal, but I would say he is relentless in terms of trying to preach his message."

Lawler had worked for Anne Flannery at PE4life since 2001. She saw his energy up close and in action many times.

"Phil is so passionate about what he believes," said Flannery. "And he never slows down. He's always looking for the latest and greatest innovation in PE that might push the needle and convince people to change how they do things."

Fellow PE pioneer Beth Kirkpatrick believes that Lawler's passion in combination with his lack of ego made him a very effective leader of the movement.

"Phil Lawler is a change agent and a leader in the profession," said Kirkpatrick. "He's a passionate speaker and persuader, but I think the main reason he's such a leader is that he's always seeking out best practice. If he finds something better, he discards what he's been doing and goes to the next thing, and that's the sign of a leader. And he's not afraid to give credit where credit is due."

If Lawler, who many called the "Father of the New PE," came across a better way of doing something, he'd change, *and* he'd tell everyone else about the better way to do it. He loved to put the spotlight on people and schools that were doing effective new things.

"Phil was always telling people about the innovative things we were doing in Titusville," says Tim McCord, PE4life Academy director in Titusville, Pennsylvania. "In fact, without Phil promoting us, we never would've been named a PE4life Academy Training Center."

"Phil is able to see the big picture," said VanLengen. "He's very passionate about what's happened at his own school for so many years, but he's

The main reason Phil is such a leader is that he's always seeking out best practice. If he finds something better, he discards what he's been doing and goes to the next thing.

willing to share with other schools around the country and to give credit when other schools make changes that deserve recognition. I think that's a big part of what Phil does that's been so helpful."

One example of his passion to spread the word is the famous Lawler PE listserv. Lawler started his listserv to let people know about all the research and best practices in the field.

"I barely know Phil," said Scott Chovanec, physical education and health department chair at Maine East High School in Park Ridge, Illinois. "Yet he touches me almost every week with his listserv. He's always sending out articles, research reports, or case studies of best practices. His listserv alone has made me a better teacher. I'm very grateful to Phil for providing that service. It shows how passionate he is about PE and what kind of person he is."

"Phil's mailing list was the catalyst for me," said Dave Kurland, head of community relations for the Chicago Bulls. "Phil is totally in tune with health and wellness news and the PE world. I have my own list that I forward Phil's e-mails to. Phil's e-mails have legs."

To be a revolutionary—to create a movement and give it the momentum needed for growth—you need to bring other people on board. Nobody ever changed a culture alone. That's where Lawler's tremendous skill as a connector came into play. The listserv he created was just one example of his ability to reach out and connect.

"Phil Lawler is a huge pioneer in this movement," said Scott Wikgren, director of physical education for Human Kinetics, a leading sports and physical activity publisher. "He's special, there's just something about him. He's a leader. He's an evangelist, the kind of guy who believes in something and enthusiastically wants to spread the word to get other people on board. A big part of Phil's charisma is that he speaks from the heart. He doesn't give you a canned presentation. He's a true evangelist.

"But what sets Phil apart is his skill set that allows him to connect people who have similar goals and put it all together so they're working together instead of separately. His greatest contribution is he's recruited people to the cause. He hasn't acted as a lone soldier."

Undoubtedly, without Lawler's amazing ability to connect with others, the entire New PE movement would be way behind where it is today.

"Phil Lawler is simply the greatest networker I've ever been around," said Zientarski. "He's able to connect dots that nobody else is able to or nobody else sees. Phil taught me to think globally."

Nobody was off limits for Phil Lawler. If he thought you could help his program or help the cause in general, he'd exhaust all avenues trying to track you down.

"Phil has a way of reading an article or seeing a television program about something that interests him, and he will just pick up the phone and call or e-mail that person for more information," said Whitthorne. "That's just Phil's way. And then, he wants you to meet his friends."

"He's willing to communicate and speak with anybody," said VanLengen. "It's helped advance this cause. Phil's ability to connect with so many different types of people—whether they're in his own profession, medical experts, business leaders, or government officials—is a special gift. He has this incredible ability to connect with and relate to people. He's able to effectively communicate what's important to him and help people see why it should be important to them as well—all in a very understanding and inoffensive way."

Lawler intuitively knew early on that he needed to build an army of like-minded people to make his vision come to fruition.

"From day one, he was always asking, 'How do we connect with more people?'" says Anne Flannery, former president and CEO of PE4life. "That was the thing that always struck me early in our relationship."

Not only was Lawler a gifted networker, he also had a special ability to get people to adopt his point of view without them thinking that their point of view was wrong.

"He has a great ability to inspire and motivate people," said Flannery. "One of the great ways I think he's been able to do that is to be very open about his imperfections and mistakes. He would say, 'This is the way I used to teach, and I had a revelation and realized I wasn't helping students get healthier and I was turning off most of the very kids I wanted to reach.' That openness has really helped him reach other people."

"Even in the early years of his new program, he reached out to parents, the school board, the medical field, community and business leaders, etc., to make sure they knew what kids were doing in his program's PE classes and why," said VanLengen. "Phil's been great at communicating to the audiences that matter; audiences that could help in some way or help enhance what he was doing."

There are a lot of great teachers who do a remarkable job in their school and surrounding community. However, Lawler had a vision that was much bigger than his local situation. He wanted to connect with people everywhere. His goal had always been to take this powerful message about exercise and learning to educators, parents, and community leaders—wherever they may be—and do it in a way that would inspire them to get involved.

"Lots of people have visions, but putting that together is a whole different story," said Zientarski. "Phil's simply able to connect dots that other people struggle to connect."

This ability to inspire people—whether they're teachers, administrators, or leaders in the community—was always one of Lawler's key strengths. He could bring others into the fold, whatever their backgrounds, and say, "Let's do this together."

"Phil reaches out to people," said Wikgren. "He asks one person to contact another person. He goes after more. The thing with Phil is that he does this because he believes in it. It started as a personal mission. It certainly was not something that was part of his job description at Naperville. He tried to create an army rather than just him out there being a 'lone soldier.' Phil recruited people to the cause and wouldn't take 'no' for an answer. He is relentless in pursuing that."

"Phil loves to connect you with like-minded people," said Flannery. "During our conversations, he kept talking about this guy named Tim McCord in Titusville, Pennsylvania, and the great things he was doing in the school district there. We ended up making Titusville one of our PE4life Academies because of that. He was great about identifying top colleagues in the field and putting PE4life in touch with them."

"Phil sees something that he thinks could help, and he delves into it nonstop. He'll talk to anyone in order to advance the cause," said Zientarski. "It doesn't matter who it is. And what really makes him effective is that he would treat President Obama the same as he does Joe Blow in lower Mississippi."

As Zientarski alludes to, part of Lawler's success story was that he saw every human being as having equal value. Amy Corner, an anxious young teacher in Arizona, attests to that.

"Phil changed my life forever," says Corner. "He lit a fire in me that was undeniable. He had me reading *SPARK,* research articles, and doing a great deal of soul searching. By the end of the year, I shocked my students, coworkers, and principal when I asked to transfer to another school to begin the work of changing physical education in my school district. I left a secure science teaching position to switch to a new school—where I didn't know anybody—to teach PE, something I'd never done before but felt was my calling. A big reason I did that is Phil's inspiration and guidance.

"Change was so scary for me. He basically held my hand every day as I was making the transition. Yet, he had never met me in person. I first saw Phil in the movie *Supersize Me.* His role in that movie was part of the inspiration I had to switch to physical education. One day, I called him up and told him what I was thinking about doing. He was so encouraging and inspirational. For a while, I was sending him e-mails more than once a day. He'd pick me up when I was having doubts or was scared. He told me there will be naysayers along the way so be persistent. I'm so glad I made the change.

"He also helped me keep things in perspective. One day I told him I was frustrated that I didn't have more face time with my students and more time for cardiovascular exercise in class. He told me my value as a PE teacher wasn't based on the number of minutes students are in class, but on what I can motivate them to do outside of class. That helped me stop putting so much pressure on myself to get so many minutes of exercise in a day."

"We can't expect to get kids fit in PE class alone," said Lawler. "Even with daily PE you need to educate them about lifestyle decisions outside of school. Todd Keating, one of our great elementary PE teachers in Naperville, spends the last minute or two of every class period challenging his students about health and wellness decisions they're going to face outside of class, at home, etc. The key is educating them enough so they pass up the convenience store on the way home from school. Or, if they do stop, they don't buy a soft drink and a giant candy bar."

Whitthorne says that one of Lawler's key motivators was his quest to find someone, somewhere, who was doing something innovative that worked.

"There is always something new with Phil in terms of his being such a great networker," said Whitthorne. "He's tapping into who's doing what and how in different parts of the country. Phil is just enthusiastic. You can't help but listen to him and understand the importance of the message."

"Phil's ability as a networker is directly tied to the fact that he believes so strongly in what he's doing that he'll call anyone, and I mean anyone, if he believes it will help the cause or grow the movement," said Costello, a former school board member in Naperville. "The other reason he connects so well with people is that you never see any ego, never see 'I know everything and you don't.' He talks with you and not down to you. Because of that, whomever he reaches out to reaches back to Phil. He can work with all kinds of people and all kinds of personalities."

According to Carrie Gibson, a long-time colleague of Lawler's at PE4life, all of Lawler's success occurred because he cared—about the cause and about people.

"Phil receives more e-mails than anyone I've ever seen, and he returns them all," said Gibson. "He responds to every obscure PE teacher in America. He gives them more information and support than they initially asked for. He helps them take it to the next level. He's the Pied Piper of PE. You hear him talk and you want to be part of this cause. He wants people from all walks of life—not just PE teachers and other educators—to get involved in this cause. He's so good with people. He can relate to anyone, from any walk of life. Once he had his epiphany and changed his approach to physical education, he got in the business of creating disciples."

"Yes, Phil's a great communicator and can be very persuasive, but I think the big reason he connects so well with people is that he cares," added Tim McCord. "He cares about people, and that comes across immediately."

Lawler's brother Dan says that one of Phil's gifts was his uncanny ability to understand where other people were coming from.

"He's terrific in his ability to relate to people. When someone doesn't get his message, it doesn't discourage him," said Dan Lawler. "He tries to fully understand the other person's point of view and address their issues. At the end of the day, he doesn't give up on changing anybody's mind. He just says to himself, 'If this isn't the right time for this person to see the potential of this cause, maybe he or she will buy into it the next time.'"

"With Phil, it isn't about what can you do for me, it's what *we* can do for kids," said Costello.

It certainly wasn't about money for Lawler. He never sought ways to benefit monetarily from his important contributions to the cause.

"Sharing his knowledge about the New PE with others—whether that's students, teachers, administrators, school board members, doctors, business leaders, politicians, whoever—brings joy to his life," said his daughter-in-law, Kathryn Lawler, who's now a physical education teacher at Madison Junior High School in Naperville. "Money has never been a driver for him."

He might not have earned much money by pursuing his passion for the New PE, but he earned the highest levels of respect from his peers in the physical education revolution.

"In my opinion, Phil Lawler single-handedly got the country looking at physical education in a new way," said Madigan. "He created a program of what every school in the country could be. Phil and Paul (Zientarski) woke up the nation. The way Phil networks people and puts them all together

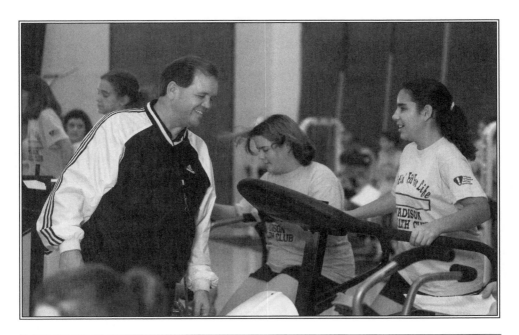

Helping kids stay motivated and encouraging them to work hard are part of being an effective physical education teacher.

is unbelievable. He is just a remarkable human being. He's not only made me a better teacher but a better human being as well."

Leave it to fellow New PE pioneer Beth Kirkpatrick to capture the essence of Phil Lawler.

"Phil Lawler is simply the most influential physical educator in the world," said Kirkpatrick. "He has a power of persuasion that few individuals have been blessed with. He is a forward thinking individual. But it is his passion, his truth seeking, his love of people, his positive thoughts for everyone, and his belief in seeking out others to join him in moving to the future, that separates him from the ordinary. He never forgets his family, and he never forgets his friends. Once you are a friend of Phil's, you are a friend for life."

◇ ◇ ◇ ◇ ◇ ◇ ◇ ◇ ◇ ◇ ◇ ◇

Phil Lawler had three passions in life: family, physical education, and baseball. And he was a tremendous success in each area.

"An amazing thing about Phil is that the PE people don't realize the tremendous impact he's had in baseball and the baseball people don't realize the amazing impact he's had in physical education," said Kevin Schmit, a long-time sportswriter in the Chicago area.

He most certainly had a positive impact in baseball. In 1997, he was inducted into the Illinois High School Baseball Coaches Association (IHSBCA) Hall of Fame. In 2009, the IHSBCA honored him with their President's Award for contributions to the sport.

Through the years, pitching became his passion within the sport he loved the most.

"He's become quite the scientist and technician when it comes to pitching," said Bill Seiple, the head coach of Naperville Central High School's baseball team.

Seiple and Lawler took over the Central team nearly three decades ago, Seiple as head coach and Lawler as his trusted assistant and pitching guru.

"He loves pitching and looking for things that might give our pitchers an edge," said Seiple. "Just as in PE, he'll call anyone on the planet to learn more about the craft of pitching. His brother Jim has been a long-time pitching coach, much of his career at Texas A&M. With Jim's help, Phil developed a relationship with Nolan Ryan built around the art of pitching."

One of Lawler's innovations at Central was the use of a three-digit code for calling pitches.

"Lawler and his catcher have the code on their forearms," said Schmit. "If Phil wants a fastball low and outside, he'll call out a three-digit number. His catcher looks at the code on his forearm and then sends the signal to the pitcher. Opponents aren't able to crack the code and pick up the pitch."

In 1976, Lawler created a summer baseball state tournament. The tournament steadily grew in size, popularity, and success. In 2009, the IHSBCA renamed the tournament the "Phil Lawler Summer Classic."

"He's had a tremendous impact in the baseball world, especially in Illinois," said Schmit. "He's long been in charge of pitchers at Naperville Central, and Central's widely known for churning out pitchers. A lot of coaches in Illinois turn to him seeking advice. Phil has no secrets. He believes in the 'brotherhood of coaching.' He is always more than willing to help other people."

Just as with physical education, Lawler always believed that coaches should embrace technology in order to coach more effectively and efficiently.

"He's been at the forefront of the technological aspects of coaching," said Schmit. "He was at the cutting edge of videotaping pitchers. Recently, due to his illness, his fellow Naperville coaches have taped pitchers in action at the school and sent the tape to Lawler online for evaluation. Lawler evaluates the pitchers on his computer and determines what they might need to change and sends his evaluation back to Central for the afternoon practice."

Perhaps his greatest impact in baseball was on the lives of the players he coached.

"Don Lichay is my favorite story about my dad's coaching," said Todd Lawler. "Lichay was the last player on the Naperville Central team his freshman and sophomore years. He was basically the team manager. However, he worked harder than anybody. Lichay would videotape himself every night—hitting and fielding—and have my dad review it. This was an almost constant practice for four years. Finally, Lichay got regular playing time as a senior, mostly due to injuries.

"After his senior season, he wanted to play college ball. My dad has great contacts in baseball, especially in Illinois. He's had a history of success in connecting with college coaches to get his Central players a place to play in college. In Lichay's case, he pushed the local four-year colleges, but nobody would take a flyer on Lichay. Until Quincy College. Quincy took him because Lichay came from a great program and my dad sold the Quincy coaches on Lichay's incredible work ethic.

"When Lichay started at Quincy, he weighed about 140 pounds soaking wet. Four years later, my dad and I saw him at a Florida Marlins tryout camp. Lichay now weighed over 200 pounds. He had a rocket arm across the diamond, great power at the plate, and ran a 6.7 60-yard dash. He was fast. Not long after that tryout, he was signed by the New York Mets and played a couple years of minor-league ball.

"Most coaches would've given up on Lichay a long time ago. But my dad believed in Lichay. He believed in helping every player maximize his talent. If a player was motivated to get better, my dad was motivated to do all he could to help him.

"I love the Donnie Lichay story. It epitomizes what my dad stands for as a person and a coach."

As a die-hard Chicago Cubs fan, Lawler's most notable baseball failure may have been that no matter how hard he cheered for his beloved Cubbies, he simply wasn't able to will them to a World Series championship.

"Phil's been a great partner and friend," said Seiple. "We've enjoyed doing baseball together. We love to tease each other, and we've helped each other. I love his passion, energy, and enthusiasm.

"There are certain people in life that you enjoy being around and who make you feel better. Phil is one of those.

"He is, and always has been, the finest baseball coach I've ever known."

7

LAWLER'S INFLUENCE GOES GLOBAL

> "**H**is passion for changing the perception of physical education, as well as the actual delivery of physical education, has changed the lives of countless children throughout the world."
>
> —*Brenda VanLengen, PE4life colleague*

Through the years, Phil Lawler always wanted to change the world of physical education as a team. Together.

At first, "together" meant getting the teachers and administrators at Madison Junior High School on the same page. Then it included motivating all the physical education teachers in Naperville School District 203 to buy in. Next, "together" meant taking the New PE message to other communities in Illinois. Before long, Lawler was on a mission to share his passion for fitness in schools with the entire country. Eventually, Lawler's New PE was expanded on, and PE4life Core Principles spread across the country.

It was only a matter of time before Lawler's messages about fitness and learning readiness began to spread around the globe. He knew that anything that helped kids become healthier, perform better academically, and have fewer disciplinary problems would have strong appeal in every country, not just the United States.

The success of the Naperville program, as well as that of other programs around the country integrating PE4life Core Principles, had resulted in growing amounts of positive media coverage. Lawler began receiving phone calls from interested parties in countries around the world. These callers wanted to learn more about PE4life, Zero-Hour PE, and other movement-based learning initiatives.

Today, the Naperville PE4life Academy Training Center has spawned a burgeoning international movement of fitness-based PE advocates around the globe. Groups from 10 foreign countries have come to Naperville 203 to learn about the district's PE4life program as well as its learning readiness PE initiatives for the classroom.

◇ ◇ ◇ ◇ ◇ ◇ ◇ ◇ ◇ ◇ ◇ ◇

Osama Al Othman is a successful businessman living in Dubai. Two years ago, he had grown concerned about the physical conditioning levels of his two daughters and was doing some research on the Internet for exercise equipment. He came across a company called Motion Fitness in Palatine, Illinois. Motion Fitness is a distributor of exergaming equipment. Al Othman spoke with Ed Kasanders, the president of Motion Fitness. He was looking for recommendations, and one of the recommendations that Kasanders gave him was to talk to Phil Lawler in Naperville, Illinois.

"I spoke with Phil for one and a half hours," said Al Othman. "What he's done with his program in Naperville and what he was promoting around the USA made my ideas concrete about what needed to be done with our children in Dubai."

Dubai, despite its Middle East location, is a very Westernized culture. The adults and children of Dubai live a very similar lifestyle to their American counterparts. That lifestyle includes a lot of fast food. McDonald's and Burger King have a significant presence. In addition, kids spend a lot of time watching television and playing video games on a PlayStation or Xbox.

In Dubai, the summers are so hot that there's virtually no outdoor activity. This exacerbates the problem of a lack of exercise. Because of cultural norms, girls are especially endangered; opportunities in sports—and even in physical education—are very limited for females.

Al Othman came to visit Naperville and was extremely impressed with the program, the facility, and just as important, the research behind it.

"What I learned from Phil Lawler impressed me so much that I decided to open an exergaming fitness center in Dubai targeting children ages 6 to 17," says Al Othman. "Once we get the kids inside our center and on the machines, we have them. They become members. They love it. Getting kids, parents, and schools to visit our center is the challenging part. The whole concept of exergaming is very new. It takes a lot of effort to explain it to people."

As Al Othman was exploring the possibility of creating an exergaming fitness center in Dubai, he would often have questions and doubts about the feasibility of the project. At these times, he'd call Lawler, and by the end of the discussion, Al Othman would be reinvigorated in his quest.

"When he talks about kids' health and exercise, he talks about it with passion," said Al Othman. "It's infectious."

Al Othman loves the exergaming approach to exercise and fitness because of the way that exergaming equipment can be customized for every individual—and how the exergaming machines treat every kid in an equitable manner.

"Soccer is the biggest sport here and a good game for fitness, but many parents pull their children out of soccer for fear of injury," says Al Othman. "Also, many kids don't like the highly competitive nature of soccer. Another problem is soccer opportunities are limited for girls. In schools, the less athletic kids feel left out of PE. The problem with sports is that too often if you are not good in sports you get left out of all physical activity.

"But with exergaming, every individual is equal. Nobody is watching you perform. There's no peer pressure to perform. The key is kids have to be entertained. They won't get on a traditional treadmill. That's why exergaming is so exciting. I had the PE teacher of some of our kids come to the fitness center, and he said, 'I've never seen these kids this active.'"

Al Othman is making a difference in the lives of young people—far across the globe from Naperville, Illinois. He says that the reason is simple: Phil Lawler.

"Phil Lawler is a treasure in the field of fitness and health," said Al Othman. "Every time I talk to him I learn something new. I appreciate and respect what he's done in his career."

◈ ◈ ◈ ◈ ◈ ◈ ◈ ◈ ◈ ◈ ◈

Dr. Christian Pfeiffer runs the Criminology Research Institute in Lower Saxony, Germany. His team includes 20 researchers in areas ranging from sociology to pedagogy. However, the institute's research explores areas that aren't always directly linked to crime.

A big area of interest for Pfeiffer is the growing gap in academic achievement between boys and girls in Germany. The performance of boys in Germany is steadily dropping.

Pfeiffer's research in this area eventually led him to Lawler. He first heard of Phil Lawler through his sister. Pfeiffer's sister had met Ratey at an international conference, and Ratey had raved about Lawler and what was being done in Naperville. At the conference, Ratey had explained how cardiovascular fitness improves not only academic performance but behavior as well.

Pfeiffer was intrigued enough by what he learned from his sister that he visited Ratey at Harvard and then traveled on to Naperville to meet Lawler and see the Naperville program.

"One of the problems we have in Germany is that boys have become obsessed with video games," says Pfeiffer. "The number of boys playing soccer and other sports has even dropped because of video games.

Even pickup soccer games among friends have dropped. Kids go home and watch TV or play video games on their computers instead of playing soccer outside."

Of particular interest to Pfeiffer's research team was the finding that youth participants in sport didn't have fewer criminal behaviors than their peers who didn't participate in sport.

"Sport doesn't seem to be the answer in lowering criminal behavior," says Pfeiffer. "Competitive behavior doesn't necessarily teach fairness. In fact, too often it teaches that winning is more important than fairness. Cardiovascular exercise seems to be the answer in terms of lowering criminal behavior. Movement is important for all students. Movement is important during the school day—including in the classroom."

A disturbing trend in Germany that Pfeiffer's institute is hoping to address is the growing learning gap *and* obesity gap between children who watched the most TV and played the most video games at an early age versus those who adopted TV and video games later.

"We're finding that those students without any type of screen—television, video game, or computer—in their rooms are healthier and perform better academically," says Pfeiffer.

Pfeiffer left Naperville with a lot of ideas that he believes are applicable in Germany. He also left town amazed at how well Lawler and Paul Zientarski played off each other in building the Naperville 203 program.

"From what I've been able to see, I think they have been the ideal combination," said Pfeiffer. "They've constantly communicated with each other. When one guy was down about something, the other guy would pick him up and say there's no way you're giving up. Here are two teachers that found flaws in the traditional sports model of physical education. They changed it, and later the academic world discovered them and their work.

"It's highly unusual to find two guys that so believed in what their vision was that they expended tremendous energy to lead this charge, in addition to their regular school duties."

Pfeiffer believes that Lawler and Zientarski have not been recognized for their work to the degree they should be.

"Phil and Paul deserve an international award," said Pfeiffer. "They should have the highest award in the field for education—not just physical education. It's my new passion to bring this benign virus I received from Phil and Paul on the importance of movement to Germany."

Lawler was thrilled with the growing interest in the Naperville program across the globe. In fact, he said that in some respects, the interest abroad was greater than domestically.

"The international interest in the Naperville 203 program and PE4life's principles of teaching physical education is at the same time exciting, surprising, and frustrating," said Lawler. "It's frustrating because the international audience seems to fully appreciate and accept the need for more fitness-based activity in education to a higher degree than educators in the United States."

One of the most impressive PE4life-related studies comes from Copenhagen, Denmark. Chris MacDonald, a professor at Copenhagen University, came to visit the Naperville 203 program and to speak with Lawler and Zientarski.

After a couple days of studying the Naperville program and talking to Lawler and Zientarski, MacDonald was sold. He returned to Copenhagen and launched a New PE pilot study at a school with 250 participating students.

For the study, physical education was increased from one day a week to five days a week. Before the study, PE consisted of sport skills and games only. For the study, a fitness-based curriculum was adopted, including running, hip-hop dancing, aerobics, bicycle spinning classes, indoor rowing, and military boot camp training. In addition, after-school physical activities were offered every day. Moreover, all junk food was removed from the school, and only healthy foods were served.

The study ran for three months, and the results were impressive. Absenteeism was down 38 percent. Concentration abilities increased 33 percent. A grade improvement of 1.5 occurred across the board. The school's teachers concluded, "The increase in exercise had great effects on classroom behavior."

Results such as these have boosted interest in the Naperville program and PE4life far outside the borders of the United States.

"We have a lot of interest from around the world now," says Zientarski. "Phil taught me to think globally."

chapter

8

A GALLANT BATTLE WITH CANCER

"**E**ven during his six-year battle with cancer, he never complained, he never asked why, he just kept accomplishing goals and being with family."

—*Scott Lawler, Phil Lawler's son*

In 2004, Phil Lawler learned that his battle to expand the New PE movement was going to have to be done while simultaneously fighting colorectal cancer. In the following six years, he went through four significant battles with the disease, including multiple surgeries and numerous rounds of chemotherapy.

As he had with challenges throughout his life, Lawler took a positive approach to his illness.

"Cancer challenges you spiritually," said Lawler. "It either takes away your faith or makes it stronger. While I've had my moments, overall it's made my faith stronger.

"I know my time will come. I just do what I can every day. These are the cards I was dealt, and I'll deal with them. The key is to live in the moment. I'll tell you what, part of my medicine is knowing I'm helping other people."

Amazingly, Lawler was always able to separate his cancer battle and personal challenges from his calling to help spread the New PE message.

"One thing that's impressed me greatly with Phil is that he's had this very serious problem—his cancer and going through chemotherapy—and I can't detect in visiting with him one iota of change in his passion and enthusiasm for what he's doing," said Cooper.

"I keep busy with my PE4life work and helping schools and teachers wherever they are," said Lawler. "Of all the medications, by far the best medicine is knowing I'm making a difference with my work."

> **O**f all the medications, by far the best medicine is knowing I'm making a difference with my work.

Lawler spent his entire life focusing on the positives and ignoring the negatives. He determined that being diagnosed with cancer wasn't going to change that approach to life.

"Cancer has actually improved the quality of my life in some ways," said Lawler. "It really helps you in terms of knowing your priorities. I used to get a lot more stressed out about traffic jams and other little things. I just laugh at them now."

Lawler had long had a lot of admirers because of the passion with which he fought for fitness-based PE and because of the classy way he did it. But the way he continued his work and reached out to help others while going through the ups and downs of four bouts with cancer really grew his legion of admirers.

"During the course of his treatment, Phil goes through ravaging treatments of chemotherapy, but he's still picking up the phone and calling me asking me if I had seen a particular story or he's shooting me an e-mail," said the Cooper Institute's Whitthorne. "Most people would be just struggling to hang on and have enough energy to speak, whereas he's still fired up. He's swinging constantly."

But the people who saw him or talked to him on a regular basis are the ones who are most impressed with how Lawler handled his cancer fight.

Anne Flannery worked with Lawler since the early days of PE4life.

"Within the last year, Phil was in the intensive care unit, and he called me to tell me he'd been able to connect with some education publication. I said, 'Phil, where are you? I thought you were in the hospital.' He said, 'I am. I'm actually still in ICU.' I said, 'What are you doing calling me?' He said, 'Well, I just had an interview.' He actually did an interview with some person while in ICU. Even in the ICU, he was calling to tell me he had just finished a 30-minute interview with some education publication about PE. That's the kind of thing where you just shake your head in amazement sometimes at his resilience and passion. He's just such a passionate advocate for quality PE."

Another long-time PE4life colleague, Brenda VanLengen, recalls Lawler's powerful ability to weave his personal health battle into speeches about the PE4life cause. She also speaks with deep admiration about how Lawler's cancer diagnosis didn't change who he was at his core. She says that he remained steadfast to his values, beliefs, and ideals.

"I remember when Phil was in front of a large audience one summer in Kingston, New York," said VanLengen. "He was speaking at a PE4life summit held there. I believe it was after he had battled cancer the first time. He talked about how his cancer battle had really illuminated how important health and quality of life is and how critical it is that we make quality, health-based PE a reality in every school so we can reach out to children and let them know about the importance of taking care of their own health. I can still vividly see him giving his speech that day and how he related his personal situation to this cause. He was so inspirational.

"A couple years later, at our first PEP grant resource conference, which was held in Naperville, Phil had either just come through his second bout with cancer or was just starting his third. It was a very emotional time, and he still got up in front of this group of people and said, 'We've been approaching PE the wrong way. It shouldn't just be about team sports. We've got to find a way to reach all children. We've got to look at ourselves and find a way we can all do this better for the good of the kids.' He was so inspirational that day as well, with his words and his passion.

Phil was a compelling and inspiring speaker. His infectious passion flowed through his words.

"I've always had a great deal of admiration and respect for Phil for all he's done and all he's accomplished and all the people he has influenced and impacted," continued VanLengen. "His reach is immeasurable. We don't know how many children's lives have been changed because of his passion. I had all of that respect and admiration for Phil before he ever started to battle cancer. Since he has faced these bouts with cancer, my admiration has only grown. And he continues to fight for what he believes in and to continue to be passionate about this cause of quality PE and doing all we can to give children the opportunity to live active and healthy lives. It's incredibly inspirational and motivational, and I appreciate Phil so much and what he's done.

"What a great role model he has been to all of us in terms of how we can fight for what we believe in. Especially if something difficult happens in our lives, how we can continue to fight the fight and battle for what we believe in no matter what our circumstances are."

Perhaps nobody was closer to Lawler from a career perspective than Paul Zientarski. For most of the latter part of their careers, they had been partners in the effort to transform PE. Although Zientarski has done many innovative things on his own to advance the New PE cause, he always looked at Lawler as an inspirational mentor—especially during Lawler's cancer battle.

"Phil's still teaching," said Zientarski with moist eyes. "He's teaching all of us how to live life in the face of adversity. He won't let this beat him mentally."

"He doesn't give up!" exclaimed his daughter-in-law, Kathryn Lawler. "He e-mailed me the day after one of his toughest treatments. He takes what's handed him and chugs along. He keeps living his life."

If anything, Lawler's battle with cancer made him even more passionate about the importance of health-and-wellness-based physical education.

"His attitude from the day he was first diagnosed with cancer has been 'I'm going to save the world while I battle cancer,'" said Zientarski. "He teaches live for the moment. What keeps the adrenalin going for Phil is the belief that he can still help people. He still offers a lot of value to the world."

On a personal level, Zientarski raves about Lawler as a friend.

"I'm very glad that Phil passed my way," said Zientarski. "I'm a much better person because of Phil. No question about it."

Lawler accepted what was out of his control and didn't waste energy labeling what came his way in life as "good" or "bad." He just dealt with it. He was driven by his values.

He lived his life by acknowledging reality and asking himself "Now what?" His answer was "Live true to yourself and your beliefs and values—no matter what, one day at a time."

"He's dealt with his life well," said his wife, Denise Lawler. "He's had a positive attitude his entire life. I think he had a lot of self-confidence and a deep faith in God instilled through his family when he was growing up."

He determined early on in his cancer battle that he wasn't going to let cancer define him; it wasn't going to take away who he was, and it wasn't going to take away his focus on the things that were most important in his life.

And it didn't.

As Ratey said, "Phil's the man. He has great courage."

9

REVVING UP THE REVOLUTION

TEN KEY FACTORS

> "**F**itness-based PE is going to change the world of education because of its positive impact on the brain, mood, behavior, and overall learning readiness of the student. And when you change education you change the world. All the world's problems are solved through education."
>
> —*Phil Lawler*

Given the growing mound of compelling research regarding exercise's positive impact on the brain, it seems inevitable that these findings will transform not only physical education but education as a whole. How quickly that happens is contingent on the rate at which key stakeholders become aware of—and fully understand—this information.

"Fitness-based physical education can make students healthier, smarter, and better behaved," said Lawler. "That's proven. It's not a theory. Now the challenge is to help every educator, school board member, and parent become aware of that fact and fully understand what it can mean for our children. Most educators still aren't aware of this powerful stuff."

We're living in a time when physical education programs are being cut or deemphasized, and new elementary schools are being built without gyms. Ironically, the exercise-based brain research that's coming out at the same time will ultimately not only save PE but also make it one of the most important subjects in schools. Quality PE and movement-based learning initiatives can be effectively and efficiently integrated into the entire school curriculum. Madison Junior High School, Naperville Central High School, and many other schools are proof of that.

"Physical education has gone from the 'Rodney Dangerfield of education' to the hub of the wheel of education," said Lawler. "The research on exercise's positive impact not only on health—which is big enough in this era of childhood obesity—but on learning readiness, as well as behavior and mood, means PE needs to be the foundation of the whole education process."

The challenge is that the majority of educators, school board members, and parents are still unaware of the research regarding exercise's positive impact on the brain. Additionally, many of those who are aware of the research are ignoring the findings, or they don't know what to do with the new information. Others are simply reluctant to change "the way we've always done things around here."

"It's a shame this movement isn't advancing faster," said Lawler. "Given the overwhelming evidence for the value of exercise in the education process, we could file a malpractice lawsuit against educators—school board members, administrators, and teachers—for not offering fitness-based PE on a more regular basis, as well as more movement initiatives in the classrooms. The problem is, too few educators are aware of the research. Awareness and understanding levels must increase dramatically."

Awareness and understanding. That brings us to 10 key factors in revving up this PE revolution. This isn't a chronological, step-by-step process. Many of these actions need to be undertaken simultaneously. As a whole, they represent Phil Lawler's approach for actualizing his vision of transforming education through fitness-based PE and movement-based learning.

1 Create Awareness in Your Community and Beyond

"It's simply a shame that more people—educators, parents, the media—don't know about the powerful research supporting exercise as a learning readiness tool," said Lawler. "What's needed is a large-scale education and communications campaign."

"The ultimate irony is that PE has been dying as a profession just as all these positive developments have been happening," says Wikgren. "Nobody changes anything without data, but now PE has the data. We need to publicize the hell out of it. Ultimately, we have to get the parents."

Lawler saw the challenge as being related to both communications and culture change. He believed that lasting culture change requires an integrated communications plan to move people along the culture change continuum: from awareness to understanding to acceptance to attitude change to behavior change.

"We need a group of key stakeholders to collectively devise a plan to help schools change their cultures as quickly as possible," said Lawler.

"The research on what exercise does for the brain is certainly going to help," said Phylis Pickett, a long-time physical education instructor in Illinois and a colleague of Lawler's in the fight for fitness-based PE. "It will speak to every administrator. Still, it's going to take a huge education and communications effort. No matter how compelling the evidence, it's still going to take a comprehensive sales effort."

Lawler and Harvard's Dr. John Ratey agreed that getting President Obama and his wife, Michelle, involved in a national campaign would help the cause immensely.

"We need to get President Obama out front talking about the importance of exercise and fitness," said Ratey.

"One thing that would really help is to get the President and First Lady actively pushing fitness and wellness lifestyles," said Lawler. "Michelle Obama's 'Let's Move' campaign looks like a good start."

Barack Obama may be the most fitness-oriented president the country has ever had. He regularly gets in a daily hour-long workout, six days a week. He alternates between weight training and cardiovascular exercise. His favorite activity is basketball, but he does a variety of cardiovascular workouts. Obama believes that turning to a fitness regimen when he was a 22-year-old student at Columbia University transformed him physically and mentally.

2 Target School Boards, Administrators, and Parents

Lawler believed that teachers—both in physical education and other subjects—are important but secondary targets in this revolution.

"Building principals are the key," said Lawler. "All the success stories we have are tied to a passionate principal who believes in the exercise for learning message. We also need to get superintendents, school board members, and parents bought in. They need to fully understand and accept that kids that are more fit not only are healthier but also more ready to learn. They also behave better in the classroom.

"Talk to any administrator in the United States today and their issues are (1) academics and standardized test scores; and (2) behavior issues—discipline problems, attendance, etc.," said Lawler. "They'd like their kids to be as healthy as possible, but what drives them are academics and behavior, because that's what they're evaluated on by school board members and parents. So, we need to talk to them speaking their language.

"Obviously, we need to keep talking to PE teachers, but we aren't going to change the PE culture through PE teachers. They weren't trained in the New PE, and they were brought up in a sports-based PE culture," said Lawler. "School boards, administrators, and parents are going to have to change the PE culture. School board members, principals, and parents are going to need to be educated, and once they're educated, they'll demand fitness-based physical education for health, learning, and behavior reasons."

Parents intuitively believe that physical activity, fitness, and academic performance are linked. In one study, 95 percent of parents said they agree that "regular, daily physical activity helps children do better academically." Lawler believed that we need to do a better job arming parents with the ammunition they need to demand more physical education and physical activity in the school setting.

Lawler also believed that parents will embrace the New PE once they fully understand it and the science behind it.

"The purpose of education is to improve the quality of life," said Lawler. "That's the universal purpose around the world. Every parent, in every country, wants to improve the quality of life for his or her kids. There's no doubt the New PE improves the quality of life.

"The cost issue will come up. What does a high-quality PE program cost? The better question is, what will it cost if we don't do it? Putting computers in every school was expensive, but it was clear that the costs would be higher if we didn't do it. The same holds true for quality wellness-based physical education."

One message that school board members and parents need to hear is that the New PE is education based and treats every student fairly and with respect. It's nothing like the military-style PE that they might remember from their own school days. Many of today's adults have bad memories of being embarrassed—or worse—in their PE classes, and those memories taint their view of physical education to this day.

Grundy Center's Beth Kirkpatrick says that humiliating activities such as dodgeball, along with humiliating and intimidating teaching tactics, need to be put to rest with the Old PE.

"The New PE has to be No Humiliation PE," says Kirkpatrick. "If students fear humiliation in the gymnasium or locker room, we'll get nowhere. We also can't intimidate and abuse kids to get them to move the way we want them to. Too many PE teachers and coaches are guilty of exercise abuse. Also, physical education should have nothing to do with competition

> **The** purpose of education is to improve the quality of life. There's no doubt the New PE improves the quality of life.

between students. For example, in the mile run, we don't need to start the whole class at the same time. That can be humiliating to the slower students, who may be working as hard or harder than the faster students based on heart rate monitor data. Stagger start them. Physical education isn't about a race."

3 Make Technology a Cornerstone of Physical Education

In Phil Lawler's mind, a couple things were givens: (1) Kids will always need to be fit; and (2) technology is here to stay.

As a result, he believed that exergaming is the future of PE—and to a large degree, the future of education in general. Exergaming combines the latest technological advances with state-of-the-art exercise equipment to provide students with a practical and enjoyable way to increase their fitness levels and cognitive functioning.

"Exergaming is the next wave in physical education," said Lawler. "We need to constantly be striving to find new ways of incorporating exercise and learning applications with kids' love of technology and gaming. Exercise, learning, and technology must go hand-in-hand as we move forward."

An exercise learning lab—like the one at Tavelli Elementary in Fort Collins, Colorado—needs to be viewed as a cutting-edge educational tool. The world of education started with a library, evolved that to a media center, and then added a computer lab. The next step is adding an exercise learning lab in every school.

"In 2008, there were nine video games bought every second," said Lawler. "Technology is here to stay. It's what our kids know. We have to capture what motivates these kids. We need to embrace it in every subject, especially in physical education. There is some amazing exergaming equipment on the market that will maximize both fitness and learning."

Technology also needs to be a big part of evaluation in physical education.

"We need to get to the point where we test 100 percent of our kids with heart rate monitors. If we don't, we have no idea what's going on inside of them," says Kirkpatrick. "Using stopwatches for PE evaluation is a third world approach. If PE teachers were in charge of transitioning us from typewriters to computers, we'd still be using typewriters."

"You don't have to start with a big budget, but you need to have a big idea," says Scott Chovanec, physical education and health department chair at Maine East High School in Park Ridge, Illinois. "Phil and Paul were my inspiration. They told me to think big and start small. Start with one class and track the data."

4 Continually Strive to Be Innovative

Former Naperville 203 school board member Tim Costello says that the core of what made Phil Lawler successful was that he always asked himself "How can we do this better?"

"Phil's advice to me from day one was to keep finding new things and new ways to keep kids engaged and active," says Kathryn Lawler, a physical education teacher at Madison Junior High School in Naperville, Illinois. "Find new equipment, create new units, etc. There's not a year that goes by that we don't change something. That all goes back to Phil's approach."

"Follow your instincts," said Lawler. "This doesn't have to be complex. Once you have the foundational philosophy—health and wellness oriented, customized goals for each student, grading on effort, variety of physical activity offerings, etc.—then make your decisions. I didn't know at the time how important getting a local cardiologist would be, or switching to small-sided games, or heart rate monitors, or customized fitness plans, or giving presentations at our open-house events, etc. I just stayed true to the basic philosophy and followed my gut from there.

"Bottom line, we need to constantly be rewriting the book on PE. It needs to be Real World PE 101, PE that makes sense to students, parents, and the public for a lifetime."

5 Incorporate More Movement in the Classroom

Ultimately, this revolution is about education, not just physical education. Yes, this New PE movement will transform physical education, but the end game needs to be a paradigm shift in the world of education as a whole.

"This whole thing isn't just about PE," said Lawler. "It's about changing the way we do education in general. And the cornerstone of that change is integrating movement into the education process—throughout the day and in the classroom."

Jean Blaydes Madigan, who heads up Action Based Learning, says that movement-based learning doesn't have to be complex for traditional classroom teachers.

"Doing lessons standing up or moving around the classroom is a good first step," says Madigan. "Movement facilitates cognition. There's plenty of neuroscience to back that up. We need to translate that knowledge to the classroom."

This isn't a movement about athletic ability or sport affinity. It's about the value of movement for every human being from a health perspective, learning perspective, and behavior or mood perspective. That knowledge is appropriate for the entire school, not just the gym.

6 Make Physical Education Part of the Scoreboard

For too long and in too many places, PE has been treated as nothing more than formalized recess. In most situations, PE is not part of a student's grade point average (GPA). Under the Old PE, there was some legitimate reasoning for that. For one, grading was biased toward the athletically inclined. With the New PE, there's no logical reason for physical education not to be part of students' GPA.

"With the Old PE model, kids and parents don't value PE," said Lawler. "They see it as formalized recess. Parents and fellow educators believe your profession and career aren't important. In addition, kids feel empowered when it comes to PE because there's no pressure from home to engage in physical education and because it's not part of the student GPA.

"A student's PE grade—if the PE program is health and wellness based—needs to be part of the student's grade point average," said Lawler. "If not, you're sending the message to students and parents that PE isn't important. PE done right is fitness based, not athletics based; it offers lifetime wellness education and is graded on effort, not athletic ability. It also includes written tests like other subjects. With those guidelines, there's absolutely no reason it shouldn't be part of a student's GPA—or the next version of No Child Left Behind for that matter. PE has to be part of GPA and No Child Left Behind in order for PE to get the respect necessary to help transform education."

"I think PE must become part of No Child Left Behind in the form of fitness-based assessments, not only to grow but simply to be saved," added Human Kinetics' Scott Wikgren.

"Unfortunately, there are a lot of poor PE programs out there, and maybe some of them should be dropped," said Lawler. "But is that the right thing to do? If we had a lot of poor reading or math programs, should we drop them? Or should we find a better way to teach reading and math? I think we—and I mean educators, parents, and community leaders—should do everything in our power to make every PE program a high-quality, wellness-based PE program. All of our children will be healthier and more ready to learn that way."

7 Constantly Emphasize the Link Between the Body and the Brain

There has long been a fairly popular perception that schools should be about "the life of the mind" and that physical activities in general—and physical education in particular—should have nothing to do with the learning process.

Given all the research data showing a positive relationship between exercise and the brain, that's simply an erroneous perception—one that's slowing down the momentum of this movement.

The reality is that the body and brain are intimately connected. When we exercise, we're not only exercising the body, but we're also stimulating the areas of the brain responsible for cognitive functioning. In fact, when we engage in cardiovascular exercise, we're actually *growing* brain cells. That's why Dr. Ratey calls exercise "Miracle-Gro for the brain."

"We must constantly reiterate that a major reason physical education and exercise should be part of every school is to enhance the learning process," said Lawler. "The growing mound of research on exercise's positive impact on the brain is why I think physical education will ultimately be the hub of the education wheel."

Dr. Ratey believes that you simply can't separate the body and the brain. They are linked in the learning process. In his book *SPARK: The Revolutionary New Science of Exercise and the Brain,* Ratey writes, "The body was designed to be pushed, and in pushing our bodies we push our brains too."

That's a statement that needs to be constantly repeated in discussions with teachers, administrators, school board members, parents, corporate executives, and other community leaders.

"We need to make a strong link between physical education, exercise, and classroom performance," said Lawler. "At Naperville Central High School, all students exercise for 30 minutes before taking standardized tests."

When you exercise your body, you're simultaneously preparing your brain for learning. It's as simple as that. There is no separation. The body and brain are one. That needs to be communicated on an ongoing basis.

"Once you have the knowledge, you have the responsibility to share it," says Madigan.

8 ▶ Get the Community Involved

"We'll never get to where we need to be with this movement without the involvement of corporate executives and other community leaders," said Lawler.

Lawler said that for years he and his PE4life colleagues focused on getting PE teachers on board first and then moving on to administrators, school board members, and community leaders. He later realized that he needed to turn that model on its head.

"It's really a three-part process," explained Lawler. "One, get community-based support—corporations, hospitals, politicians, etc.; two, get buy-in from principals and school board members; and three, get the teachers on board. Ideally, it happens in that order, although every situation is going to be different."

"If I've learned anything from my time with PE4life, it's that nobody can do this by themselves," says Flannery, former CEO of PE4life. "We need to do it collectively and innovatively. We all need partners—and corporations are especially important."

Consider the creative working relationship between the Chicago Bulls and the Noble Network of Charter Schools in Chicago.

"We were really looking for a way to make an impact in schools," says Dave Kurland, the Bulls director of community relations. "As part of the Noble Street Charter School, we've developed a school curriculum that will include PE twice a day for 40 minutes; 80 minutes of PE per day. The school believes in the importance of physical education so much that you have to pass a fitness assessment to move on to the next grade.

"Phil Lawler's inspirational stories about how PE has transformed kids are what really inspired me to push for this project. Once I showed just a little interest, Phil kept after me."

"The unique thing about schools is they hold the future employees of our companies," said Lawler. "Given the shape of kids today, our companies can't afford to hire this next generation for health care reasons alone. The corporate world needs to work with us to solve this problem."

As an organization, PE4life agrees. The critical first step in every community that PE4life enters is a community meeting that brings all the local stakeholders together—school administrators and board members, influential community leaders, foundations, and businesses.

"We have to continually keep this issue in front of business leaders," says VanLengen. "They need to look at their bottom lines and realize that their health care costs are out of control and their productivity is down. When they look at the next generation, they see a group that's even less healthy, which means rising health care costs and less productivity. We need to push them to action to help fund better quality PE."

"This is an education challenge and a funding challenge," said Lawler. "We need more and more people spreading the message about how fit kids are smarter, better behaved, and healthier. Moreover, we need corporate America to fully understand what this all means for their futures and the future of this country. If the movement's going to continue—let alone speed up—we're going to need corporate dollars and encouragement."

9 Revamp College Programs for Physical Education Teachers

Naperville Central's Paul Zientarski believes that in order for the revolution to speed up, the movement needs a Phil Lawler–type champion at the university level—someone who'll passionately push for a "New PE" way of preparing young PE teachers.

Lawler wholeheartedly agreed.

"We have to get the university people, the professors who are preparing the next generation of physical education teachers, to teach a health-and-wellness-based approach to PE," said Lawler.

Today, the majority of the prep programs for PE teachers at colleges and universities across the United States still emphasize skill development and a team sport model versus fitness and lifestyle education. In an environment where childhood obesity rates are growing and overall fitness levels are declining, a health and wellness model must be the focus of PE training programs in order for physical education to meet the needs of 21st-century students.

"They don't teach the fitness approach to PE in college," says Kathryn Lawler. "My student teaching experience here in Naperville shaped who I am as a teacher. It laid the foundation for the rest of my career. As hard as it is to believe, I didn't see a heart rate monitor or TriFIT machine while in college."

"Our national association, NASPE (National Association for Sport and Physical Education), has to become more fitness and health based instead of sport skills based," said Phil Lawler. "We really need to think about what our exit goals are for K-12 physical education. In a country where only 3 percent of adults over the age of 24 get their primary physical activity from sports, does a skill- and sports-based PE model make sense?"

"Fitness should absolutely be number one on the list of priorities for PE teachers," says Ratey. "We need to rattle the cages of these professors that are preparing the next generation of PE teachers."

"It's really about lifestyle education, not physical education," according to Kirkpatrick. "It's all about how to live a healthy lifestyle."

"Whatever health care reform we ultimately end up with in this country, whatever we do, it won't work until we change the way we live," adds VanLengen.

Lawler contended that we need to stop looking at physical education as a way to develop athletes.

"Our athletically inclined kids will become athletes through our country's extensive youth sports system—especially with the growth of club sports organizations," said Lawler. "We don't have to worry about developing athletes through PE.

"PE teachers—every teacher for that matter—should ask themselves each morning, 'What am I teaching today that will help these students the rest of their lives?' I'm a big fan of the 'Enduring Understanding' concept. Basically, this concept asks you, as an educator, to ask yourself 'Am I teaching something that's important for my students today?' And more importantly, 'Is it something that will positively impact my students for the rest of their lives?' If you're teaching the New PE, I think a PE teacher can easily say yes to that question.

"Now, if you're teaching the Old PE, and focusing on sports skills and team sports competition and how high the volleyball net is, etc., I don't think you can honestly answer 'yes' to that question," said Lawler. "Under the Enduring Understanding concept—which is part of the whole Understanding by Design (UBD) philosophy—the Old PE falls way short. Is there any other subject as far off track in schools as Old PE?"

10 Research to Drive the Revolution

As Rick Schupbach, director of the PE4life Academy Training Center in Grundy Center, Iowa, says, "Data drives decisions."

Without research supporting the New PE philosophy and highlighting the benefits of exercise for academic performance, there will never be enough momentum to result in a paradigm shift in the world of education.

"Research gives us credibility," said Lawler. "Without the data from the first heart rate monitor I used on that girl during our Mile Run Day, I never would've had the epiphany that drove the rest of my career. We must utilize the growing mound of research on exercise and the brain, and we must collect data within our own programs if we're going to change the way things are done in physical education and education as a whole.

"The bottom line is, without legitimate research data, our school systems won't change, and our kids won't enjoy the numerous benefits of physical activity during their school years and beyond. We must all be aware of the emerging research in this area and constantly communicate it. It's our responsibility as educators. And it's equally as important that we become researchers and data collectors within our own programs so that we can justify the New PE, as well as movement-based learning programs in our schools.

"We don't need to become college-level research scientists, but we do need to know how to measure the effectiveness of what we do."

Passion will carry the message and champion the cause, but it's research—and the communication of that research—that will change the culture of education.

Lawler believed that if these 10 factors are undertaken in earnest, we can speed up this revolution and positively enhance the lives of more kids.

"I've spent an ungodly amount of time on the phone over the last 20 years trying to speed up this revolution," said Lawler. "I've had countless phone calls. First, they were mostly with people in Illinois, then across the country, and in the last couple years, with people interested in a PE4life-type program around the world.

"Despite all my efforts, and the efforts of hundreds of my colleagues and fellow advocates, too many educators around the country are thinking, *We don't need PE anymore. It doesn't have any long-term value. We need to focus on core academics,*" said Lawler. "I would bet that 97 percent of the country is still closer to the Old PE than they are the New PE. That's completely unacceptable given the powerful research demonstrating the benefits of exercise in a learning environment.

"What we have created is the future, and the future is now," said Lawler about his Naperville program and the other PE4life programs across the country. "This is how PE has to look everywhere. We can do it. We just need to work together to make it happen. As corny as it may sound, it's time to really get moving!"

EPILOGUE

> **"T**hat's all a man can hope for during his lifetime—to set an example—and when he is dead, to be an inspiration for history."
>
> —*William McKinley*

The newspaper article said he lost.

Todd Lawler begged to differ.

"I actually read an article this week that said my dad lost his battle with cancer," said Lawler at his dad's funeral. "He didn't lose to cancer—the cancer died. He won."

So true. The cancer died on April 23, 2010. Phil Lawler was the winner. He beat cancer.

He beat it because he never let the cancer change who he was. He maintained his faith and was true to his values until his last breath.

He beat it because through his attitude and actions he told cancer, "You may eventually get my body, but you're not touching my spirit. You're not touching my passions or the true essence of who I am."

He beat it because during his battle with cancer he taught us how to both live and die: Stay in the moment. Focus on *today,* what you can contribute *today,* how you can love *today.* Yesterday's gone and tomorrow will take care of itself. Live *today.*

Make no mistake about it, Phil won. His spirit beat the cancer.

Undoubtedly, Phil Lawler was a winner in the ways of the world. He received numerous awards and honors, including being named a first-team selection on *USA Today*'s All-USA Teacher Team and being inducted into the Illinois High School Baseball Coaches Association Hall of Fame. He was recognized as the "Father of the New PE." He won a state championship as a baseball coach. He was featured glowingly in numerous newspaper articles and television features.

But more important, he was an even bigger winner in the ways of the spirit.

He loved to help people find solutions to problems, to overcome obstacles in their lives—whatever those obstacles were. And he truly loved helping kids, whether it was helping baseball players find a place to play in college or teaching his less athletically inclined students that there were plenty of fun ways they could be physically active besides team sports.

Phil Lawler cared. He gave all he had to others. Not in a financial sense but a spiritual sense. He gave his talents, his passion, his ear, and his heart to others—all the way to the end.

He also found a cause much bigger than himself. It was a cause he devoted most of the second half of his life to: finding ways to motivate kids to move their bodies so the quality of their lives could be enhanced in many ways.

He started a revolution. It continues to grow. And the world will be a better place because of it.

◇ ◈ ◇ ◈ ◇ ◈ ◇ ◈ ◇ ◈ ◇ ◈ ◇

April 29, 2010.

Hundreds of people come one by one to St. Elizabeth Seton Catholic Church in Naperville, Illinois. For more than five hours they come, slowly passing Lawler's open casket, many of them kneeling to pray or silently saying a few final words to a man they greatly admire. The line is made up of people whom Lawler positively affected: former students, teaching colleagues, community leaders, high school and college baseball players— many in uniform (Phil would've loved that)—and friends and admirers . . . lots and lots of friends and admirers. It's a quiet setting. The visitors use hushed voices to tell each other, and to tell the Lawler family, what Phil meant to them.

At Tavelli Elementary, 900 miles away in Fort Collins, Colorado, the scene is much louder. Over the course of five hours, a couple hundred kids—30 at a time—are passing through an exercise learning lab inspired by Phil Lawler. The lab is filled with boisterous kids having fun while simultaneously exercising and learning. They are playing games on interactive machines that stimulate their bodies and brains. After 30 minutes in the lab, they head back to their classroom, as the next class of students files into the lab. Back in their classroom, the kids are energized. Their brains are in an ideal state of learning readiness.

Similar scenes play out in 42 states and 10 foreign countries on this day. From Denmark to Dubai, from Florida to California, Phil Lawler's legacy of fitness-based physical education and classroom-based movement initiatives lives on.

Yes, that newspaper article had it all wrong.

Phil Lawler didn't lose his battle with cancer. The cancer died. Phil won. His spirit is alive and well.

It's most definitely alive and well . . .

AFTERWORD

By

John J. Ratey, MD,
associate clinical professor of psychiatry at Harvard Medical School
and author of *SPARK: The Revolutionary New Science
of Exercise and the Brain*

I have met very few people who have had a greater impact on the world than Phil Lawler. That's heady praise I know, but this middle school physical education teacher ignited a movement that is revolutionizing education.

Lawler's passionate quest to transform physical education in order to help kids lead healthier, more productive, and more satisfying lives was simply inspirational. Phil Lawler was a hero, and he was the driving force behind a revolution that's changing the world. Its effects will ultimately be felt well beyond the walls of our classrooms.

That said, progress is often slower than we'd like. Daily, wellness-based physical education is still the exception rather than the rule in the United States. Too many stigmas, misunderstandings, and misconceptions about physical education are still out there.

Perhaps the greatest fallacy in American education today is that dropping physical education will improve academic performance.

Too many schools across the country have fallen into the trap of marginalizing or eliminating PE because of mounting pressures to improve academic test scores as a result of No Child Left Behind. This is a disturbing trend in light of the growing evidence citing exercise's positive impact on the brain, as well as studies demonstrating that fit students achieve more academically.

The bottom line is, physical education and traditional academic subjects such as reading, math, and science are complementary, not contradictory. Exercise is the one thing we know optimizes brain function. Not only does exercise improve blood flow and immediately elevate the neurotransmitters driving our mood and focus, it also acts like Miracle-Gro for the brain. Research has found that as little as three hours a week of aerobic exercise increases the brain's volume of gray matter (neurons) and white matter (connections between neurons).

The building block of learning is the wiring together of brain cells or neurons. Physical exercise facilitates this wiring by stimulating the production and release of a number of key chemicals such as BDNF, a protein that encourages brain cells to wire together and multiply. Therefore, cardiovascular activity results in increased brain functioning during cognitively challenging tasks. Simply put, students are more ready to learn after exercise.

The good news continues. The positive effects of exercise in a learning environment go beyond increasing brain volume. Exercise has also been shown to improve attention span and focus, to lower anxiety and depression levels, and to result in fewer discipline incidents—all factors that affect learning. After students exercise, they are less impulsive. Their motivation to learn is increased, and they have less desire to get out of their chairs and move around.

To maximize the benefits of physical education, physical education philosophies and curriculums must evolve from being based on skills to being based on health and wellness. Too many schools still have an outmoded approach to physical education centered on team sports and humiliating activities such as dodgeball. The emphasis in physical education needs to be on developing healthy lifestyles, including individual fitness goals for *all students,* not just the athletically inclined.

Cutting PE in an effort to improve academic test scores is simply ill-conceived and counterproductive. We now have plenty of ammunition to build the case for daily, health-and-fitness-based physical education in every school (K-12) across America.

The fitness movement is picking up steam; it has the potential to be bigger than the anti-smoking revolution. But your help is still needed. There are a variety of things that any citizen can do, whether it's writing a letter to your state or federal representative, making a speech at your local school board meeting, or encouraging your company to form a collaborative wellness-based partnership with the local school district. The list goes on. Assess what you can do and get involved. You *can* make a difference.

Phil Lawler is a perfect example of the tremendous impact one person can have. Your efforts certainly don't need to be as far reaching as Phil's, but they can definitely speed up this important revolution.

Phil's counting on you. Join the movement. Help change the game.

APPENDIX

"The whole world is following in your footsteps my friend," said Dr. John Ratey, author of *SPARK: The Revolutionary New Science of Exercise and the Brain,* in a 2009 letter to Phil Lawler. "You started a revolution that has its own steam now. It was your vision that changed the paradigm. You are a hero Phil, and we are all in your debt as professionals and people. You have changed the world."

"Today, they're coming from all over the world to study what's being done in Naperville, a program started by Phil Lawler," says Dr. Kenneth Cooper, the "Father of Aerobics." "His influence has spread across the globe. Phil Lawler is legendary."

Phil Lawler didn't start out on his quest in order to become famous. He did it for the cause. He believed that he'd found a way to improve the lives of young people—to really make a difference.

Temple Grandin—a highly acclaimed professor, author, and speaker—was once asked what she thought the meaning of life was. Her answer was profound:

"When I was younger, I was looking for this magic meaning of life. It's very simple now. Making the lives of others better doing something of lasting value. That's the meaning of life; it's that simple."

Phil Lawler epitomized that. Given that definition, few people's lives have been as meaningful as Phil Lawler's. He made very little money from his calling. He wasn't rewarded with any significant material comforts for what he did for kids. But his growing impact on students' lives around the world is immeasurable.

As Grandin would say, that's what life is all about.

Phil Lawler's burial service was held on April 30, 2010, at St. Elizabeth Seton Catholic Church in Naperville, Illinois. It was a beautiful service, highlighted by five remarkable eulogies that perfectly captured Lawler's essence. The eulogies were from Paul Zientarski, Bill Seiple, Kim Marino, Todd Lawler, and Scott Lawler. The following are excerpts from those eulogies. After these remarks, excerpts are presented from tributes by two of Lawler's PE4life colleagues, Brenda VanLengen and Rick Schupbach.

Remarks from Paul Zientarski,
physical education department chair,
Naperville Central High School

Phil Lawler was an advocate.

He took tremendous pride in his profession. He constantly preached the importance of teaching PE the right way. . . .

Phil Lawler was a networker.

This was truly Phil's gift. He reached out to people from all over the country and the world. Once he got in touch with you, he never lost touch. Everyone became wound up in his web. He kept connecting the dots and putting people in touch with others in his network. Before there was an Internet and e-mails, Phil had a phone. He continued making those phone calls right up to the end. . . .

Phil Lawler was a motivator.

If you ever encountered Phil—even as a stranger—your first impression was "This man has enthusiasm!" You couldn't help but feel his excitement, for whatever he was doing or had just learned. . . .

Phil Lawler was class.

I never heard Phil curse in the 25 years I knew him. He always wanted to do things first class, and that is exactly what he did. . . .

Phil Lawler was an innovator.

He was constantly coming up with something new, and he would spread those innovations to anyone who was willing to listen and try them. . . .

Phil Lawler was a talker.

When Phil called or walked into my office, I knew it was going to be an hour of stimulating discussion about a new item he'd come across or someone interesting he'd recently spoken with.

The only thing that slowed down during his six-year battle with cancer was the office visits. The upside was the phone calls increased in frequency. E-mails went from 1 a day to sometimes as many as 12 a day. The school district often scolded him because his e-mails were taking up too much space on the district servers. . . .

Phil Lawler was a teacher.

Phil not only taught his students but also taught teachers about the New PE. He influenced not only current teachers but future PE teachers as well. . . .

Phil Lawler was a friend.

Most of all, Phil Lawler was my very dear friend. Of all the things I'll cherish in my memory of Phil, the best thing is that he thought of me as his friend. To say that I'll miss him is an understatement, but I was blessed to have known him and call him my friend. . . .

The measure of a man is if he can leave the world a better place than when he entered it.

Phil, you did a great job.

Remarks from Bill Seiple,
head baseball coach at Naperville Central High School

Here are "Phil's Five." Five things that Philip used to say to our players over the years.

1. Failure is one step closer to success.
2. There's no excuse to be outhustled.
3. Practice doesn't make perfect. Practice makes permanent. Perfect practice makes perfect.
4. Focus on those things you can control.
5. Master the changeup.

I've decided that perhaps I could honor Philip's memory today by offering up another "Phil's Five" for all his family and friends that are here today celebrating his life.

1. *Call someone you care for and talk for a long time with them.* Magicians do their magic with wands. Phil did his with the telephone. I bet Philip had many good friends that he never even saw face to face. Perhaps we could all use this sad day to call that sibling we're mad at or that old friend that you haven't spoken to in many years—and make their days better. Phil would have liked that. . . .

2. *Get your family and take a trip to Iowa.* I'm convinced that Philip knew just about everyone who lived in Iowa. He also was pretty familiar with everyone who went to school in Iowa. And, I think he was working on everyone who actually drove through Iowa. He was proud to have come from a little town in the western part of the state, once known for popcorn and Andy Williams. And now forever known as the childhood home of Phil Lawler.

3. *Remember, it isn't the position you hold but what you do with the position.* Philip was a junior high school physical education teacher and a high school baseball coach. And I would bet that he thought those two endeavors were the two most important jobs in the world. Naperville Central baseball and physical education were the vehicles for Phil's passion. No offense to all the talented people here today, but I believe that he was the very best at what he did. . . . Some people see things for what they are. Philip had the gift of seeing things for what they could be.

4. *Treat everyone with respect, regardless of who they are.* I didn't see Philip get mad too often, but he absolutely hated to get big-timed. He hated it because he had no frame of reference for it. . . . Phil didn't understand getting talked down to because he didn't do it himself.

5. *When the day is done, try to make sure that everything and everyone you touch is better for it.* Philip led a life of enhancement. Virtually everyone he touched was enriched by his conversation, his encouragement, his support, and his love. . . . I believe a lot of us would agree, that after talking with Phil, you felt a little better, a little more important.

For the past 35 years, I have been privileged to call Philip my friend. We shared a passion for the game, for our players, for our community, and for our families. If the measure of a man is the quality of his friends, nobody stands taller than I do today.

Phil, I love you and I already miss you.

Remarks from Kim Marino, Phil Lawler's daughter

Looking out I see many family and friends . . . It is such a healing gift to be surrounded by your love for my father. . . .

I have struggled to find the right words, the right stories, the right note that would speak truly of my father . . . But there are simply too many . . . *Family, faith, baseball, coaching, physical education* . . . All words that hold a lifetime connection to my dad. He had a rich life, a giving life, and a life that I admired even to his last breath . . .

My father loved unconditionally, it didn't matter what you did or didn't do, and it didn't matter what the color of your skin was or how old you were . . . It didn't matter what opinion you held, or if you played baseball or not . . . What a valuable gift I saw in my father's attitude. My dad loved and was loved. Who could ask for anything more?

I only hope I can be as strong . . . that I can be as generous in my love as he was in his abundant love for life and family.

I love you, Dad . . .

Remarks from Todd Lawler, Phil Lawler's son

I have to thank everyone for so many things these last couple of days. There has been an outpouring of support for our family, and that is greatly appreciated.

"Win" was his last clear word to me, and that is what he did his whole life. In everything he did, he was a winner. Whether it was PE, baseball, or family. He won. He won in everything he did.

I actually read an article this week that said my dad lost his battle with cancer. He didn't lose to cancer—the cancer died. He won.

A great man once told me your future and legacy is decided by what you do in the moment. My dad lived in the moment . . . When you were talking with him, there was nothing else more important than the conversation he was having with you . . . He wasn't thinking about what he had to do that day or what might be going wrong . . . He was focused on *you,* and that is what made him special.

He was God's servant. He was a visionary. He had passion. He had charisma. But words can't really describe who he was.

All I know is my father was an incredible man in so many ways. He opened his heart and poured out all his passion . . .

I am the luckiest kid alive to be able to call this great man not only my dad but my hero. I stand here PROUD.

We all need to keep his spirit alive . . .

I love you, Dad.

Remarks from Scott Lawler, Phil Lawler's son

My dad had a strong faith. He was a man of few words when it came to his faith. Saying my dad was a man of few words about anything is odd I know. But he was a man of action, not words, when it came to his faith. He lived his faith by the way he treated those around him.

Even during his six-year battle with cancer, he never complained, he never asked why, he just kept accomplishing goals and being with family . . . And I think it's important for people to know that my mother was every bit as strong as my dad during those six years. . . .

Dad had a passion for physical education.

He loved heart rate monitors. He's probably in heaven right now trying to convince Jesus to strap on a heart rate monitor!

Dad had a passion for baseball.

I remember when I was in middle school, everyone used to tell me I'd be a coach and teacher some day like my father and uncle. I never thought that would be true. I thought I'd try my hand at something else. But the influence of my father and uncle led me to coaching and teaching. [He's now the associate head coach at Notre Dame.]

Dad's favorite movie, *Field of Dreams,* is now mine too. Not because it takes place in my dad's birthplace of Iowa, or even because it's about baseball. It's my favorite movie because of the final scene showing a father and a son playing catch.

I can't wait to play catch with you in heaven, Dad. I'll do my best to be a good person and make sure I see you there.

Excerpt from a poem written as a tribute to Phil Lawler by Rick Schupbach, Lawler's PE4life colleague

Life is a journey that passes us by . . . in what seems like just a glance
Especially when special people are placed in it . . . and join us in the
    dance

Life brought me one of those particular people . . . who inspired me as
    none before
And I viewed him as a unique gift . . . because he touched me at my core

A mentor, a friend, a colleague . . . whose advice was always so sound
Those close to me understand . . . his role in my life has been profound

I trust my life's work shows a passion . . . for others to see and feel each
    day
And may it serve as a reflection of his impact on me . . . in a small yet
    significant way

Each night I take time to thank God . . . for the blessings I have received
    that day
Included always will be my good friend Phil Lawler . . . whose life
    showed us all a better way

Excerpt from a tribute to Phil Lawler written by Brenda VanLengen, Lawler's PE4life colleague

Have you ever thought about what you'd like people to say about you at your funeral? The end of your life may not be something you want to think about, but the way you live your life will be your legacy.

Yesterday, I attended the funeral of a man who I've known for nine years, but who will impact my life forever. But more importantly, the way he lived his life will impact millions of lives.

At the funeral, Phil Lawler was remembered for his faith, his devotion to his family, and his passion for his life work in physical education and baseball. . . .

Phil started his career as a gym teacher and coach, similar to many former athletes. He taught PE for half his career believing that all kids liked sports as much as he did. His PE classes had the typical emphasis on team sports. . . .

But midcareer he examined the way he and his colleagues were delivering physical education and realized that they needed to do more to reach all children, not just the athletically inclined. He changed his philosophy to introduce a wide variety of sports and fitness activities to engage more children. . . .

He utilized technology to connect with kids on their level, using heart rate monitors to give children feedback on what was happening within their bodies. He searched out high-tech games that allowed children to pedal within a video game or dance on high-tech dance pads. . . .

He wasn't the only innovative PE teacher in the country, but he was one that really took a bold stand about including *all* children in PE. He created a high-quality approach to PE that is now known as the "New PE."

His passion for changing the perception of physical education, as well as the actual delivery of physical education, has changed the lives of countless children throughout the world.

He became friends with Dr. Kenneth Cooper, the "Father of Aerobics," and Dr. John Ratey, a noted brain researcher from Harvard. He appeared in the movie *Supersize Me* and spoke in front of Congress. He made phone call after phone call to members of Congress, state legislators, corporate executives, medical professionals, school administrators, and physical education professionals throughout the world.

Phil turned 60 in February, and his time on Earth was far shorter than any of us hoped it would be. However, Phil lived each of those 60 years to the fullest. He lived his life with purpose, with passion, and with integrity.

When it comes time for each of us to have our lives recounted, will we be able to have the same said?

RESOURCES

All URLs are accessible from the PE4life website: www.pe4life.org (in the Research section).

Physical Activity and Health:
A Report of the Surgeon General Executive Summary

This article suggests that the *amount* of physical activity is more important than the intensity. It states that physical activity could include briskly walking for 30 minutes, mowing the lawn for 30 minutes, running for 15 minutes, and so on. Everyone can benefit from physical activity. Significant benefits can be obtained by including a moderate amount of physical activity in your life. Physical activity also improves mental health and relieves symptoms of depression and anxiety.

> Manley, A.F. (1999). Introduction, summary, and chapter conclusions. Physical activity and health: A report of the Surgeon General executive summary (pp. 9-14). Washington, DC: Centers for Disease Control and Prevention.

Promoting the Participation of Children With Disabilities
in Sports, Recreation, and Physical Activities

This report discusses the impact of physical activity on children with disabilities. Exercising has been shown to increase health and slow the progression of chronic diseases for children with disabilities. Along with the health benefits, physical activity can have tremendous effects on a child's psychological well-being. Participating in physical activity or sports gives a child opportunities for friendship, creative expression, and the development of a sense of identity and a purpose in life. Special Olympics participants show higher self-esteem, more physical competence, and more independence. The report also states that mildly strenuous exercise can help reduce maladaptive behaviors and fatigue in children with autism and other developmental disabilities. This report suggests that you should focus on including children with disabilities instead of excluding them.

> Murphy, N., Carbone, P., & Council on Children With Disabilities. (2008). Promoting the participation of children with disabilities in sports, recreation, and physical activities. *Pediatrics* 121(5). www.pediatrics.org.

Exercise: An Alternative ADHD Treatment

This article describes how exercise can affect children with ADHD. Dr. John Ratey explains how exercise affects the brain. Exercise increases dopamine and norepinephrine, which are associated with regulating the attention system. If a person exercises regularly, this increases the baseline levels of dopamine and norepinephrine. This article argues that exercise balances alertness, movement, and emotions. It also describes a study that found that walking at least three days a week for six months increased the volume in the prefrontal cortex. The prefrontal cortex is in charge of impulses, planning, and inhibition. This article suggests that physical activity can improve attention and the ability to control impulses as well as decrease the symptoms of ADHD.

Ratey, J. (2008). Exercise: An alternative ADHD treatment. ADDitudeMag.com. www.additudemag.com.

Physical Education, School Physical Activity, School Sports, and Academic Performance

This study reviewed the relationship between academic achievement and school-based physical activity. The study is a compilation of general studies that show the positive relationship between physical activity and academic achievement. The review of all the articles suggests that there is definitely a relationship between the two.

Trudeau, F., & Shephard, R. (2008). Physical education, school physical activity, school sports, and academic performance. *International Journal of Behavioral Nutrition and Physical Activity* 5(10).

Physical Activity and Student Performance at School

Provided within this article is a comprehensive review of several articles that research physical activity. The review includes the experimental designs and the outcomes of each study. Most, if not all, of the studies conclude that physical activity positively affects academic achievement.

Taras, H. (2005). Physical activity and student performance at school. *Journal of School Health* 75(6), 214-218.

Exercise and Working Memory: An Individual Differences Investigation

Researchers tested whether students who already had a certain level of brain function could be affected by physical activity. The participants included college students. The method used in the study required the participants to exercise for 30 minutes before performing the academic tasks (memory tasks). The study found that exercise might be more beneficial for those with lower achievement scores. This could be because children, who score lower in working memory, have a tendency to be more distracted than people with higher working memory.

This shows that exercise has an effect on both attention and working memory.

Sibley, B., & Beilock, S. (2007). Exercise and working memory: An individual differences investigation. *Journal of Sport and Exercise Psychology* 29, 783-791.

Physical Fitness and Academic Achievement in Third- and Fifth-Grade Students

This study tested whether exercise had an influence on academic performance of preadolescent children. The study looked at math scores and reading comprehension. Researchers tested the fitness levels with the Fitnessgram. They found that physical fitness was positively related to academic achievement. For all three academic tests, the participants who had lower BMI or were more fit had better test scores.

Castelli, D., Hillman, C., Buck, S., & Erwin, H. (2007). Physical fitness and academic achievement in third- and fifth-grade students. *Journal of Sport & Exercise Physiology* 29, 239-252.

Aerobic Fitness and Cognitive Development: Event-Related Brain Potential and Task Performance Indices of Executive Control in Preadolescent Children

This study was conducted to find out if exercise affected executive control in preadolescent children. Executive control refers to the processes of the brain that include perception, memory, and attention. This study used a test that tested attention and the ability to filter useless information, called interference. The researchers found that exercise was related to better brain function. Students who participated in the exercise group improved their response time compared to the control group. Another finding was that the children with higher fitness levels had higher response accuracy compared to the lower-fit children in all conditions. These findings suggest that children with higher fitness have improved attention and ability to inhibit unimportant information.

Hillman, C., Buck, S., Themanson, J., Pontifex, M., & Castelli, D. (2009). Aerobic fitness and cognitive development: Event-related brain potential and task performance indices of executive control in preadolescent children. *Developmental Psychology* 45(1), 114-129.

Physical Fitness and Academic Achievement

This study researched the effect of exercise on academic achievement. The study found that the mean achievement scores improved along with the overall fitness scores. The tests for academic achievement covered math and reading comprehension for every fitness level. From fit to unfit, academic scores improved with exercise. In terms of socioeconomic status (SES), fitness and academic scores increased at a greater rate for students with higher SES than for those with lower SES. This suggests that students with lower SES might have extra factors that affect their academic performance.

Grissom, J.B. (2005). Physical fitness and academic achievement. *Journal of Exercise Physiology* 8(1). www.science.smith.edu.

Exercise Is Positively Related to Adolescents' Relationships and Academics

In the study described in this article, the results suggested that exercise could lead to better relationships for adolescents, including better relationships with their parents. The researchers also found that children are less likely to participate in exercise if they don't have social support.

Field, T., Diego, M., & Sanders, C. (2001). Exercise is positively related to adolescents' relationships and academics. *ADOLESCENCE* 36(141), 105-110.

Physical Activity and Sedentary Behavior Patterns Are Associated With Selected Adolescent Health Risk Behaviors

This study investigated the relationship between physical activity and adolescent risk behaviors. The participants who exercised more than five times a week were less likely to have sexual intercourse, smoke, get drunk frequently, and be truant. They were also less likely to have low self-esteem. The academic article describes wide-ranging results that support the belief that physical activity has a positive impact on children's well-being.

Nelson, M., & Gordon-Larsen, P. (2006). Physical activity and sedentary behavior patterns are associated with selected adolescent health risk behaviors. *Pediatrics* 114, 1281-1290.

The Influence of Physical Activity on Mental Well-Being

This report is about how physical activity affects mental well-being. One of the major statements in this article is that physical activity decreases the risk of developing depression. Experiments show that exercise can help treat depression symptoms. Studies also indicate that exercise can have moderate effects that may help reduce anxiety symptoms. It is believed that exercise energizes people and produces more positive attitudes. The emotional benefits are greater if the individuals set personal goals for themselves. In terms of physical activity, self-esteem is important to study because of its close association with emotional stability and because low self-esteem is related to poor health behaviors.

Fox, K.R. (1999). The influence of physical activity on mental well-being. *Public Health Nutrition* 2(3a), 411-418.

The Relation Between Physical Activity and Mental Health Among Hispanic and Non-Hispanic White Adolescents

This article claims that physical activity is associated with a positive mood, greater self-esteem, and greater physical and psychological well-being. Physical activity was shown to have an impact on decreasing the feelings of sadness and suicidal ideation among Hispanic and non-Hispanic white students. Higher levels of vigorous physical activity were associated with a decrease in planning suicide.

> Brosnahan, J., Steffen, L., Lytle, L., Patterson, J., & Boostrom, A. (2004). The relation between physical activity and mental health among Hispanic and non-Hispanic white adolescents. *Archives of Pediatrics & Adolescent Medicine* 158, 818-823.

The Role of Schools in Preventing Childhood Obesity

This report provides advice on what a school's role should be in promoting the health of children. Most schools can help students adopt and maintain healthy eating and physical activity behavior. One step that this article suggests is electing a school health coordinator to help promote a health and wellness program in your school. Before you start the program, you need to assess your school's current program or your needs for the program. Once the assessment is done, your school needs to develop a plan to strengthen the school's policies on nutrition and physical activity. Policies should include having high-quality courses of study for health and physical education, but also creating a wellness promotion program for school staff. In the development of new courses, an administrator or educator should consider emphasizing knowledge and skills for promoting a lifetime of physical activity. Courses should meet the needs of students and keep the students active for the majority of PE class time. You need to make it enjoyable for all students. In addition, you must give students opportunities for physical activities outside the gym. Give the students other options for physical activity.

> Wechsler, H., McKenna, M.L., & Lee, S.M. (2004, December). The role of schools in preventing childhood obesity. *The State Education Standard* 5(2). www.cdc.gov/HealthyYouth/physicalactivity/pdf/roleofschools_obesity.pdf.

Be Smart, Exercise Your Heart: Exercise Effect on Brain and Cognition

This article discusses a literature review of various studies that show the positive relationship between physical activity and brain function. The article identifies many articles about research on adolescents, adults, and animals and how physical activity affects them. This quote sums up the article entirely: ". . . there is converging evidence at the molecular, cellular, behavioral and systems levels that physical activity participation is beneficial to cognition. Such evidence highlights the importance of promoting physical activity across the lifespan to reverse recent obesity and disease trends, as well as to prevent or reverse cognitive and neural decline. Accordingly, physical activity can serve to promote health and function in individuals, while also lessening the health and economic burden placed on society."

Hillman, C.H., Erickson, K.I., & Kramer, A.F. (2008). Be smart, exercise your heart: Exercise effect on brain and cognition. *Perspectives* 9, 58-65.

ABOUT THE AUTHOR

Ken Reed is a sport, fitness, and education consultant. He is the author of PE4life's "Blueprint for Change," an overview of the physical education landscape and a 10-step action plan for physical education stakeholders. In addition, he is an award-winning columnist (focusing on sport issues) and teaches a variety of college-level sport studies courses. He is the author of *Sara's Big Challenge,* a novel targeting sport-oriented girls ages 10 to 14. Reed holds a doctorate in physical education and sport administration. He lives in Littleton, Colorado, with his wife, Sandy, and two daughters, Lexi and Angi.

ABOUT PE4LIFE

> "PE4life has a proven record of reversing the trend in this country of inactivity by increasing physical education, which has been proven to impact students' ability to learn."
>
> —Tom Harkin, U.S. Senator

PE4life is a regionally focused nonprofit organization with national reach and is dedicated to developing a country of active and healthy children and youth by increasing access to quality physical education. PE4life promotes making physical activity fun and interactive to engage all students. PE4life partners with community, business, and school leaders to facilitate systemic change in the perception and delivery of physical education with the desire to improve the health and wellness of children through quality physical education. PE4life offers professional development and support to educators and administrators who desire to create positive change in their schools and communities.

Programs incorporating PE4life's Core Principles employ today's best practices in physical education to inspire and educate all students about the fundamental importance of lifetime physical activity and fitness. PE4life has worked successfully in schools with diverse student populations in a variety of settings. Regardless of the environment, PE4life has been able to support those individuals and groups who wish to be a catalyst for positive change.

The six PE4life Academy Training Centers represent a broad spectrum of students and PE programs. Centers are located in Kansas City, Missouri; Grundy Center, Iowa; Indianapolis, Indiana; Titusville, Pennsylvania; and Rogers, Arkansas. PE4life has also added model sites in regions of expansion to further influence schools and to allow people to observe PE4life's Core Principles in action.

Our Reach

To date, PE4life Program Services have trained 360 teams with over 3,000 educators, administrators, and community leaders from 39 states across the country, affecting 2,855 schools and reaching over 2.2 million children.

In the 2009 to 2010 school year, PE4life Program Services trained 87 teams with 888 educators, administrators, and community leaders from 10 states across the country, affecting 278 schools and reaching over 320,000 children.

In the 2008 to 2009 school year, PE4life Program Services trained 38 teams with 524 educators, administrators, and community leaders from 13 states across the country, affecting 179 schools and reaching over 100,000 children.

What Makes Us Unique?

PE4life supports getting kids active and healthy by engaging them through fun and interaction. We invite implementation of technology into physical education classrooms by encouraging the use of interactive gaming, heart rate monitors, pedometers, and other feedback tools.

Enabling students to monitor their heart rate allows them to observe the direct effect exercise has on the body. Whether they are using interactive gaming equipment or participating in sport, fitness, or adventure activities, students learn how to maintain the appropriate intensity of activity to enhance their health. PE4life supports physical educators and connects them to appropriate resources to enhance the delivery and results of their program.

Assessment is a key component to a successful program. PE4life advocates for the incorporation of assessment tools, which can help students and teachers track progress made toward achieving fitness goals. By using innovation and technology to evaluate, plan, and monitor a student's progress, programs incorporating PE4life's Core Principles are having a positive impact on the health of children.

PE4life Core Principles

We believe that a quality physical education program should do the following:

- Offer a variety of fitness, sport, leisure, and adventure activities to all students.
- Implement a K-12 standards-based curriculum.
- Provide a safe and encouraging learning environment.
- Use individual assessments.
- Incorporate current technology.
- Extend PE beyond the walls of the gymnasium.
- Ideally, be offered to every child every day.

For more information about PE4life, please visit www.pe4life.org.